HAUNTS OF MACKINAC

Ghost Stories, Legends, & Tragic Tales of
Mackinac Island

Todd Clements

House of Hawthorne Publishing
Grosse Pointe, Michigan

Haunts of Mackinac
Ghost Stories, Legends, & Tragic Tales of Mackinac Island
by Todd Clements

ISBN-10: 0-9786641-6-7
ISBN-13: 978-0-9786641-6-9

Library of Congress Control Number: 2006929075

Published by:
House of Hawthorne Publishing Company
P.O. Box 36985
Grosse Pointe, Michigan 48236

ACKNOWLEDGEMENTS

I want to thank all those who helped make this book a reality no matter how small a part. I appreciate all the time and cooperation I was given by believers and skeptics alike.

Thanks go out to: Nina, Zach, Catherine, Mom, Mom C., Graham, Theresa, Jeff, Josh, Lisa, Doc, Jacob, Coleen, Julie, Patty, Brad, Dick, Michelle, Pat, Kelly, Diane, Karleen, Erin, Steve, Cindy, David, Laura, Katie, Clint, Bruce, Ward, Paul, Glenn, Jody, Phil, Timothy, The City of Mackinac Island, The City of St. Ignace, Mackinac State Historic Parks, The Mackinac Island Library, The St. Ignace Library, The Mackinac Island Tourism Bureau, The Bentley Historical Library, and all others who have been a part of this endeavor.

DISCLAIMER

The stories in this book are for entertainment purposes only. Although the ghost stories in this book are considered "true and accurate," the subject of ghost stories falls into the realm of legends and folklore. Therefore, no claims to their authenticity or basis in fact are made. Those who read this book are expected to make up their own minds as to each story's believability.

I have attempted to relay the historical facts of each story, to you the reader, to the best of my ability. However, some of the stories lacked the historical documentation required. Therefore, some of the information used was provided by individuals who are familiar with certain locations' histories, but not necessarily considered experts on them.

It is encouraged, for those who wish, to seek out the ghosts of Mackinac Island. However, please never trespass on private property and do not engage in activities that could be considered unwise or dangerous. Otherwise, please enjoy both this book and your adventures while on Mackinac Island.

CONTENTS

Dedicated To The Memory of My Dad.

WHAT IS A GHOST

Science has yet to come up with a concrete explanation for ghostly activity, but many people agree that they do exist. So what or who are ghosts, why are they here, and where can they be found? This chapter will give you the basic knowledge needed to understand ghostly phenomena.

What is a ghost and when are they most commonly found?

All living and non-living material is made up of atoms. These atoms produce an electromagnetic field. It is believed that these electromagnetic fields are the basic building blocks for ghostly activity. Although there may not be a physical presence of a person or object, its electromagnetic form, or "aura", may be present. However, an electromagnetic form needs the proper conditions to manifest into a semi-physical state; what we call a ghost. Some of the environmental conditions that favor ghostly activity are:

1. *Low moisture or humidity levels.* These levels are usually found in arid locations and northern regions in the fall and winter months.
2. *An electrically charged atmosphere or area.* A location where thunderstorms or other natural electrical sources are present.
3. *Solar flare activity.* When the Sun produces a large solar flare, some of the energy can reach Earth.
4. *Geomagnetic storms.* Strong solar winds off the Sun can reach Earth and cause variations in the magnetic field (cause of The Northern Lights).
5. *A new or full Moon.* Has an effect on the Earth's magnetic field.

6. *A nearby electrical source.* A source of electrical power such as a plug or outlet on a wall.
7. *Silent areas.* In a quiet place, you will be more likely to hear any unusual noises (i.e. footsteps).

In addition to the environmental conditions listed above, an equally important component of a ghostly encounter is the human factor. Some people have a natural sensitivity to ghostly activity and therefore are more likely to have an "experience." In addition, those who had a relationship with the person, while they were alive, may be more "connected" to them after they die.

Although not all of these conditions need to be met to produce a ghost, the more the better. The popular notion of a northern hemisphere Halloween fits the conditions you want to find. The cool dry air, a thunderstorm on the horizon, a full moon, and the emotional electricity create a perfect setting for a ghostly encounter.

Either way, the likelihood of having an encounter with a ghost is left to chance. Under the right conditions, however, your luck may improve.

Where are ghosts most common?

Ghosts can be found throughout the world. However, some locations tend to be more active than others. Good environmental conditions are important for ghostly sightings, but the location's history is the most important factor. Ghosts tend to haunt places they knew in life. These familiar places seem to draw them. Regardless of why, ghosts commonly haunt two types of locations.

The first location is the scene of a tragic event. A crime scene, battlefield, the location of a suicide, or fatal accident is great place to find paranormal activity.

Ghosts can also have a strong emotional or physical attachment to an area or place. For example, a woman weeping over the graves of her children or a ghost returning to its childhood homestead where fond memories were had.

Why do ghosts haunt?

A ghost does not know it is dead.
Death can come to us at any time and at any place. Sometimes it happens so fast a person does not realize they died. This cause for a ghostly presence is common with murders and accidents. These ghosts also can be very young children, who are confused or lost.

Unfinished Business
Some people are as determined in death as they were in life to complete a task. This can be as simple as saying goodbye to loved ones to making sure that unfinished business is completed. Once this is done, they can move on.

Materialistic Attachment
The reason for this ghostly presence is an attachment to someone, something, or someplace. They just do not want to let go of the "thing" they had in life. Ghosts typically will remain until they come to an understanding that they are dead and material attachments are meaningless.

Messenger
Some ghosts appear in order to deliver a message to the living. The message, often to a loved one, can be one of comfort or warning. Messengers typically do not continue to haunt after the message has been delivered.

Vengeance

The reason for this type of ghostly presence is similar to those with unfinished business, except the reason is revenge. This ghost is looking to bring justice to those who crossed them in the past.

In what way can ghosts manifest themselves?

Ghosts tend to manifest as a representation of their own self-image or how they are remembered. They do this through smells, sounds, by moving objects, and/or by materializing before our eyes.

Ghost Smells

A ghostly smell is somehow connected to the ghost producing it. For example, the perfume they wore, or the cigarettes they smoked. However, not all ghost smells are good. Some can be quite foul such as rotting flesh. These types of smells are usually related to an evil or non-human entity.

Ghost Sounds

Ghost sounds are some of the most common phenomena experienced by witnesses. One theory for this is that sound requires less energy to create than other forms of manifestation. Ghosts can make sounds similar to the living and these sounds can range from footsteps to actual voices.

The intensity of sound can vary as well. Some sounds will be identical to real earthly noises, others will be undetectable to the unaided ear. In these cases, recording equipment is used to pick up the sounds and amplify them.

Ghosts Moving Objects

Some ghosts actually have the ability to move material objects. The extent to which a ghost can move an object varies greatly. In some cases, objects move only inches over a long period of time. In others, the objects can quickly fly across a room, sometimes smashing into a wall. The difference in the way an object moves is due to the amount of energy available and how skilled the ghost is in using it. Typically, the objects moved are small, such as a pen. However, there are cases, highlighted within this book, in which much larger objects, such as furniture, have been moved. In most instances of a ghost moving objects, the witness is not involved. Still, there are several tales where a ghost has jerked the bed sheets right off a sleeping guest.

Visual Ghosts

The least frequent, but most sought after type of manifestation is the visual ghost. The amount of energy required to manifest as a visual apparition is believed to be substantial. However, as a ghost's manifestation progresses and energy is collected, the visual ghost may also produce smells, sounds, and/or move objects.

What types of ghosts are there?

Freeform Apparitions

Freeform apparitions or ghosts are exactly that; they take no defined form. These types of ghost can be difficult to recognize and are commonly misidentified. Many real world explanations can account for misidentified freeform apparitions. For example, dust caught on film, smoke from a cigarette, or a person's breath in the cold. However, there are those unexplainable cases in which the freeform apparition is actually a ghost. Several types of freeform apparitions exist. The following are the most commonly observed.

Orbs: Usually appear in video recordings and photographs as balls of light. These images can include tails emitting from the orb indicating motion (Plasmoids) or can appear as unexplainable lines of light (Streamers).

Mist: This type of ghost, also known as ectoplasm, appears as a smoky fog floating in the air. It can range from white to gray in color and may be capable of becoming a full apparition.

Shadows: A rare form of ghost, a shadow, can appear as either freeform or a full apparition. These type of ghosts tend to be difficult to spot as they blend in with other natural shadows.

Ghost Lights: This type of ghost appears as a glowing light usually at a distance from those witnessing it. Science has attempted to dismiss these lights as swamp gas, ball lightning, or something else explainable. However, there are cases in which the source of the light cannot be scientifically explained.

Full Apparitions
Whether it is a person, animal, ship, etc., full apparitions take on a recognizable form. In some cases, full apparitions can appear to be so real that the witness does not realize they are seeing a ghost until it vanishes right in front of their eyes.

Full apparitions are believed to require a large amount of energy in order to manifest. Therefore, it is possible that the full apparition, with limited energy resources to draw on, will only partially appear. A witness, for example, may see a human apparition in which only the upper half of the body is visible.

As for ghostly objects such as ships, their appearance seems to be connected to the person(s) who died onboard. Some of these object sightings have been described as looking the way they did when they ceased to exist. Could this have something to do with the last memories of those associated with the object?

Sentient Spirits

The sentient spirit is well aware of who, where, and why it is there. Taking either a freeform or full apparition appearance, these ghosts have the ability, albeit limited, to interact with living people. There are even cases of these ghosts holding long conversations with a living witness.

Poltergeists

The English translation of the German word poltergeist is "noisy ghost." However, in addition to making noise, poltergeists can also produce smells, move objects, and, in very rare cases, produce a form of apparition.

Currently, there is much debate over what exactly is a poltergeist. Some believe it is a powerful ghost attached to a person, place, or thing. Another belief is that it is not a ghost at all, but the product of a person with psychic abilities. The latter school of thought states that the person, unknowingly, has psychically created all of the ghostly phenomena themselves.

Historical Repeaters or Imprints

The historical repeater, like the poltergeist, is currently a hotly contested topic. Some feel that this phenomenon is explainable as a strange, but natural event. For example, ball lightning. The theory states that conscious energy is produced during highly emotional events and can be trapped or recorded. How this happens is still a mystery, but some feel that certain types of rock, such as limestone and quartz, tend to produce the effect more often.

During a historical repeater, a witness may experience the sights, sounds, and even smells from another time. Think of this encounter as a three dimensional video playing on a loop around a witness. Historical repeaters rarely, if ever, interact with the living. The historical repeater is also known as a residual haunting or an imprint.

Non-human Entities

This type of ghost is considered less common than the human variety, but they do exist. Non-human entities are just that, non-human; they never were a living human being. These ghostly presences can range from angels to demons, or animals to ships.

HAUNTING & GHOST ACTIVITY SCALES

At the end of each story that contains ghosts, you will find a _Haunts & Ghost Activity Scale._ This scale is provided to give you a better idea of the reported level of ghostly activity found at the story's location.

(Time Scale) Most recent reported sighting
- ★   In the distant past (over 20 years ago)
- ★★   In the recent past (within the past 20 years)
- ★★★ Ongoing (current sightings)

(Intensity) Strength of the activity
- ✳   Minor (cold spots, smells, flickering lights)
- ✳✳   Moderate (sounds, orbs)
- ✳✳✳ Major (apparitions, objects moving)

(Regularity) Frequency of activity
- ✳   Rarely
- ✳✳   Occasionally
- ✳✳✳ Common

THE STRAITS OF MACKINAC

A View of the Straits of Mackinac

The Straits of Mackinac have long been regarded by sea goers as one of the most dangerous bodies of water in the world. The high concentration of lighthouses and foghorns found here gives magnitude to the dangers a ship faces in these straits. Along with hazardous islands, shoals and shallows, the straits can produce perilous weather that can rival some hurricanes. These storms can generate unforgiving gales, thick fog, and icy waters with little or no warning. These treacherous conditions have claimed the lives of many who have traveled through the Straits of Mackinac.

The Ghost of Waugoshance Lighthouse

Waugoshance Lighthouse

Brief History:

Built in 1851 and standing 76 feet above the straits, this solemn giant was in service until 1912. During the lighthouse's 61 years, it warned many ships of the dangers in the area. The lighthouse was run by several keepers during its operation. It also was the victim of Lake Michigan's weather and was under relentless repairs. In 1883, the outer walls of the lighthouse were encased in an iron shell that protected it from the elements for almost 100 years.

In 1887, John Herman arrived at the lighthouse. John was a heavy drinker and fond of practical jokes. For five years, he served as an assistant keeper. Then in 1892, he was promoted to head keeper. One night at the turn of the century, John, being the prankster he was, locked his assistant in the lighthouse's lantern room at the top of the tower. By the time the assistant was able to unlock the door, there was no sign of John anywhere. It is thought that John, in a drunken state, must have fallen off the lighthouse into the water and drowned. Some of the keepers that followed John Herman reported unexplainable events taking place at the lighthouse. Until 1912, most of the 15 keepers and their assistants either transferred or resigned from Waugoshance Lighthouse.

In 1912 the lighthouse was decommissioned and abandoned. However, during World War II the lighthouse was utilized for target practice. Many pilots and their crew unloaded bombs and gunfire at the old lighthouse during simulated military bombing runs.

Today, the Waugoshance Lighthouse is abandoned and in need of many repairs. Fortunately, The Waugoshance Lighthouse Preservation Society is currently working to restore the lighthouse to its former glory.

Ghostly Activity:

After the mysterious disappearance of John Herman in 1900, his replacements reported numerous events that could not be explained. There were stories of chairs being kicked out from under people and reports of the lighthouse boiler mysteriously filling with coal. Until the lighthouse was replaced by Gray's Reef and White Shoal's Lighthouses in 1912, it was difficult to find a willing keeper to tend the lighthouse, as they all feared the ghostly pranks of John Herman.

Waugoshance's Haunting & Ghostly Activity Scale:
Time Scale: ★

Intensity: ★ ★ ★

Regularity: ✹

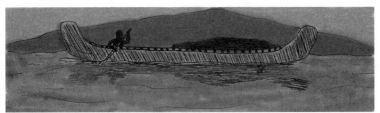

A Sketch of Sebastian's Journey

Sebastian's Quest

During the mid-seventeen hundreds, Detroit, Michigan, was a French settlement. One particular Frenchman, by the name of Sebastian, was engaged to marry a woman named Zoe in the spring. Before they would marry, however, he went to northern Michigan to hunt for furs, promising to return as soon as the ice melted from the lakes. Unfortunately, Sebastian never returned to Zoe. The story goes on to say that Zoe waited by the edge of the Detroit river day after day for her love to return. Suddenly one day she saw him on the water with furs piled high on his canoe. As he came closer to her, he vanished into thin air. Every year Zoe returned to the edge of the river and every year the ghost of her lover returned, only to vanish again.

The final resting place of Sebastian and his canoe have never been found. It is assumed that he came to his end in the Straits of Mackinac. Today, the ghost of Sebastian is still seen in both the Straits of Mackinac and on the banks of the Detroit River. It is believed that Sebastian is still trying to return to his Zoe.

Sebastian's Haunting & Ghostly Activity Scale:
Time Scale: ★ ★
Intensity: ✱ ✱ ✱
Regularity: ✱

A Sketch of The Griffon.

The Griffon

Brief History:

    The first commercial and decked ship to sail the upper Great Lakes was The Griffon, also known as "Le Grifon." The ship was built during the summer of 1679 under direction of the famous explorers Robert Cavelier Sieur de LaSalle and Moise Hillaret. The Griffon was designed as a French brig weighing around 60 tons with a length of seventy feet from bow to stern and a width of sixteen feet. She was the largest ship, at the time, to sail up into the Great Lakes. Powered by two sail masts and armed with seven light guns, this superior ship was designed to help LaSalle gain a strong foothold in the fur trade and dominate the industry in the northern trade route.

On August 7, 1679, the Griffon was completed and set sail from Cayuga Creek, near Niagara Falls, for the northern reaches of the Great Lakes. Her crew consisted of thirty-four men including LaSalle, Lieutenant Tonty, Father Hennepen, two other missionaries named , La Ribourde and Membre', the pilot Luc La Dane, and twenty-eight others.

The first historic event that occurred on the Griffon's maiden voyage was the naming, by Father Hennepen, of the body of water north of the Detroit River. Hennepen decided that the lake should be named after Saint Claire, whose feast day fell on August 11, the day they arrived. LaSalle broke a bottle of wine over the bow of the Griffon christening the new lake. From that day forward the body of water was known as "Lac Ste. Claire", or today as Lake St. Clair.

While the Griffon sailed through Lake Huron, she was caught in a severe storm through which LaSalle believed the ship and crew would not survive. Records show that LaSalle had told the crew they were all "undone" and feared they would not survive the storm. The entire crew, except the pilot Luc, fell to their knees and started to pray for their lives. Luc, however, was determined not to die in a "nasty lake" when he had challenged and survived many storms as an oceangoing pilot. As you will learn, fate would, in time, catch up with him.

The Griffon reached the mission, at what is now St. Ignace, on August 27, 1679. While there, LaSalle learned that two members of an advance group had deserted and were in Sault Sainte Marie. LaSalle did not have the time to search for the deserters, so instead, he left Lt. Tonty along with twenty men to establish a trading post and search for the deserters. He instructed his trusted second in command to arrest the deserters once they were found. Lt. Tonty was then to proceed with the deserters to Green Bay, Wisconsin where the rest of the group would be waiting.

Robert Cavelier Sieur de LaSalle.

During the first week of September, the Griffon arrived in Green Bay. While there, the ship was stocked with as many furs as it could hold. Although the ship was ready to return, LaSalle was not comfortable sending the ship back without Lt. Tonty onboard, so LaSalle delayed the departure in hope that Lt. Tonty would arrive soon. However, LaSalle was later notified that Lt. Tonty was caught in stormy weather and it would take him some time to reach the Griffon. LaSalle could no longer justify delaying the Griffon's departure, especially considering the ship's full cargo and the debts he owed in Niagara. Thus, the Griffon departed with only a skeleton crew onboard, the pilot Luc and five others.

The Griffon was last seen by Indians in the northern reaches of Lake Michigan. The Indians advised the pilot, Luc, to stay near the shore because the Straits of Mackinac had many shallows and shoals that the ship could strike. The fate of the Griffon after this meeting is debatable. Many believe the ship came into a severe storm and sank with her crew onboard. Others speculate that the crew either stole the furs and sank the Griffon or the crew was murdered by a group of Indians who stole anything of value and set the ship afire. Soon after the Griffon disappeared, several furs washed up on the shores of Mackinac Island. It is thought to be all that was left of the famous Griffon.

Ghostly Activity:

Regardless of how the Griffon and her crew perished, their ghosts continue to sail the Great Lakes. There are reported sightings of a phantom French brig-style ship traveling through the Straits of Mackinac. Many believe this ship is the ghost of LaSalle's Griffon. Are the six crewmembers and their ghost ship still trying to reach their destination?

Some, who report seeing the Griffon's ghost, describe her as being on an eastbound course, with no visible crew on her decks. The ship slowly vanishes the closer it gets to those who witness it. The best time to attempt to see the Griffon's ghost is on foggy mornings. The place to watch from the Island is along the coast facing the Mackinac Bridge.

The Griffon's Haunting & Ghostly Activity Scale:

Time Scale: ★ ★
Intensity: ✷ ✷ ✷
Regularity: ✷

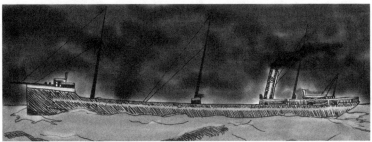

A Sketch of the W. H. Gilcher

W. H. Gilcher

Brief History:

One of the first steel-hulled ships to sail the Great Lakes was the W.H. Gilcher. Built in 1891 by the Cleveland Ship Building Company, she was the sister ship of the Western Reserve. Both ships were thought to be unsinkable and the finest example of shipbuilding at the time.

However, on August 30, 1892 the sister ship, The Western Reserve, went down just north of Whitefish Point during a heavy storm on Lake Superior. The sole survivor was a sailor named Harry Stewart. Unfortunately, the crew of the W. H. Gilcher would have no survivors to tell her tale.

At three hundred and two feet, built at a cost of $200,000 (about $3,500,000 today), the W. H. Gilcher was a large but sturdy steel steam ship. Holding the record for the largest load of wheat ever carried by a ship of her time, she was a vessel of which to be proud of. However, on a routine trip to Milwaukee with a payload of coal, the Gilcher would perish.

W. H. Gilcher's Capitan Lloyd Weeks was an expert sailor in the Great Lakes whose abilities were never questioned. J. C. Gilchrist, a principle owner of the W. H. Gilcher, once said, "Capitan Weeks, who sailed her, was one of the best captains on the lakes."

The Crew of the W. H. Gilcher included many men from the Cleveland area, the same region as those onboard the ill-fated Western Reserve. This was a very sad time for many families in the Cleveland area who were just recovering from the previous loss.

Just two months after the tragic loss of her sister ship, the W. H. Gilcher came to a terrible end. She sits in the waters on the western side of the Straits of Mackinac. The exact details of what caused the W. H. Gilcher to founder are not completely clear.

The weather in the Straits of Mackinac on the night of October 28, 1892 was severe and the waters very rough. In fact, the storms that night lead to the sinking of many ships throughout the Great Lakes. High winds from the storm, with gusts in excess of 60 mph, not only caused trouble at sea, but also left damage over several states, and spread a fire in the city of Milwaukee which cost the city around $7,500,000 (about $150,000,000 today).

No matter how the W.H. Gilcher sank, weather played some role in the accident. Some believe the ship's steel bent and broke allowing water to flood the ship and sink it. Others feel that a one hundred forty foot schooner named the Ostrich under the command of Capitan McKay collided with the W. H. Gilcher. The Ostrich sunk the same day at roughly the same time as the W.H. Gilcher. Unfortunately, the entire crew of six onboard the Ostrich were killed as well.

The last people to see the W. H. Gilcher were the Capitan of The Waukesha and Capitan Duncan Buchanan of the Schooner Seaman. The Waukesha's Captain reportedly saw the lights of the W. H. Gilcher suddenly go out while Capitan Buchanan, who was the last known person to see the Gilcher, saw the ship trying desperately to survive the storm. Later that night the Schooner John Shaw reported sailing through the remains of either The Ostrich, W. H. Gilcher, or both.

Over the next few days, wreckage washed ashore on High and North Manitou Islands. Most of the debris was from the wooden schooner Ostrich that was believed to have been completely destroyed during the storm. However, Capitan Stuffelbaum discovered string backs from the W. H. Gilcher, which held down the canvas covers on the lifeboats. Apparently, the string backs had been cut with some haste as the ship sank. Regrettably, no lifeboats were found and it is believed that the crew did not have enough time to free them from the doomed Gilcher.

The crew that was onboard the W. H. Gilcher when she went down is as follows: Capitan Lloyd H. Weeks, First Mate Ed H. Porter, Second Mate Harvey Peters, Chief Engineer Sydney Jones, Thomas Finley, Charles Thompson, Charles Hunton, Albert Green, Charles Green, William Hostler, George Hostler, Wilson Carr, Peter Schakett, C.E. Williams, Mr. Faulhaber, and Fred King. Several of the crewmen were new to the ship and their identities went down with the ship.

Ghostly Activity:

Today, the lost crew of the W. H. Gilcher still sails through the Straits of Mackinac. When the fog rolls in, many people have reported seeing the ghostly shadow of the ship moving through the waters near Mackinac Island. Others have heard the eerie horn of the ship blowing at night to warn other ships of her presence.

Another mysterious fact is that the three ships which last saw the W.H. Gilcher also became shipwrecks themselves, all sinking within a few weeks of the anniversary of the W. H. Gilcher's tragic end.

A freighter sailing through the foggy Straits of Mackinac.

W. H. Gilcher's Haunting & Ghostly Activity Scale:
Time Scale: ★★
Intensity: ✳✳✳
Regularity: ✳

Deadly Shipwrecks

In the search for ghosts and paranormal activity, one of the best places to look is the location of a sudden death or tragic event. Therefore, included are the tales of the known deadly shipwrecks within the Straits of Mackinac.

Shipwrecks are found throughout the Straits of Mackinac. However, only a few of those wrecks took the lives of sailors aboard. The following shipwrecks are those in which this tragedy occurred.

Deadly Shipwreck Map

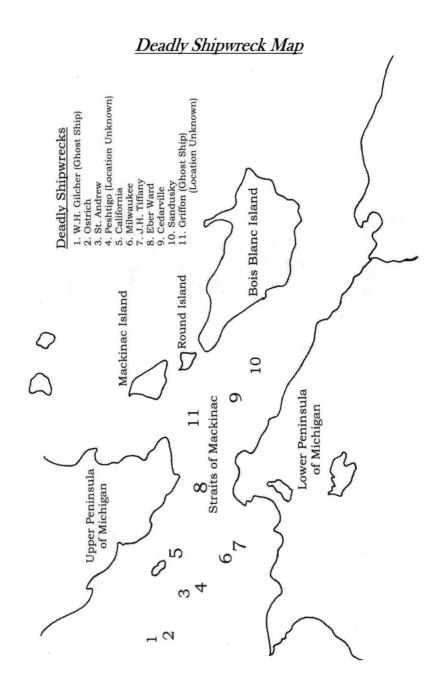

Deadly Shipwrecks

1. W.H. Gilcher (Ghost Ship)
2. Ostrich
3. St. Andrew
4. Peshtigo (Location Unknown)
5. California
6. Milwaukee
7. J.H. Tiffany
8. Eber Ward
9. Cedarville
10. Sandusky
11. Griffon (Ghost Ship)
    (Location Unknown)

Sandusky

Built: 1848
Sank: September 20, 1856
Size: Length 110'
Width 26'
Cause of Shipwreck: Storm
Crew Lost: 7 (all hands)

The brig Sandusky now rests at the bottom of the Mackinac Straits in 83' of water. Many divers have said that it is one of the finest shipwrecks to explore in all the Great Lakes.

Before the Sandusky arrived at her final resting place, she was in the service of several owners over an eight-year period. The final owner of the ship purchased her days before she sank and had come to have disagreements with several members of the crew. Two of these crewmembers, Charles O'Shea and Samuel McQue, decided to desert the ship under the new ownership in Chicago. They were soon arrested by local authorities and placed in the custody of the Sandusky's captain, Thomas Smith. The two deserters were forced to board the Sandusky and sail with her. Unknown to them at the time, they would receive a death sentence for their capture.

On September 16, 1856, the Sandusky set sail for Buffalo, New York with a crew of six and a payload of grain. Under Captain Thomas Smith, she had made it through Lake Michigan and into the Straits of Mackinac. While in the straits, full gale winds and a severe storm would doom the Sandusky and her crew.

As the ship began to sink into the water, a nearby brig, The Columbia, with Captain Wells at the helm, was unable to maneuver and aid the Sandusky. Helpless to save the crew of the Sandusky, the crew of the Columbia watched her go down. Three initial survivors of the Sandusky's sinking hung from the ship's mast, which remained above the turbulent waters. The high winds kept all sailing vessels from attempting a rescue, so a side-wheeler called the Queen City under the command of Captain Watts was sent to save the three remaining Sandusky crewmembers. Unfortunately, the waters were too rough for the Queen City to get to the survivors in time. When the Queen City arrived, the weather, wind, and waves of the straits had claimed the three men from the mast they clung to.

J.H. Tiffany

Built: 1856
Sank: November 29, 1859
Size: Length 137'
Width: 27'
Cause of Shipwreck: Collision
Crew Lost: 5

The J.H. Tiffany was sailing westward on the night of November 29, 1859. Just after midnight, a ship named Milwaukee, was entering the straits heading eastward with another ship, the Free State, close by.

A few moments later, the Free State crossed in front of the Milwaukee and obstructed her view. At the same time the J. H. Tiffany was heading westward directly in the path of the Milwaukee. The two ships could not see each other. The Free State just missed a collision with the J. H. Tiffany. However, when the Free State cleared the way, the Milwaukee and the J. H. Tiffany were destine to collide.

At about 12:30 am the two ships crashed into each other. The Milwaukee sank quickly and the 30 people onboard had just enough time to launch the lifeboats.

Everyone on the Milwaukee managed to survive the accident, but the crew of the J. H. Tiffany would not be so lucky.

The J. H. Tiffany managed to stay afloat longer than the Milwaukee, but this would eventually doom some of the crew. Captain Monroe Turner of the J.H. Tiffany tried to beach the ship on a nearby reef. Unfortunately, his ship could not make it that far.

The Free State had lost sight of the J. H. Tiffany, making rescue difficult. As the ship sank, the crew struggled to get high on the masts, with the hope that the depth of the water was less than the height they had climbed. As more of the crew ascended the mast of the sinking ship, it broke sending all those on it into the cold waters below. In the struggle to swim to the foremast, which was still above water, several of the desperate crew drowned.

The crewmembers who survived were: Captain Monroe Turner; First Mate Joel Turner; Seamen Fredrick Mellon, John M. Smith, and Henry Merritt. Those who did not survive were: Second Mate Henry E. Graves; Cook William Thompson; Seamen George Smith, James Swail, and John Lupton. John Lupton, only 25 years old, was engaged and would have been married as soon as he returned.

The last person involved with the J.H. Tiffany to die was a salvager named William Wright. He was on a dive and surfaced with the bends (decompression sickness); he died soon after.

Cedarville

Built: 1927
Sank: May 7, 1965
Size: Length 588'
Width: 60'
Height: 22'
Cause of Shipwreck: Collision
Crew Lost: 10

The Cedarville was built in 1927 by Great Lakes Engineering Works of River Rouge, Michigan. Owned by U.S. Steel Corporation and Captained by Martin Joppich, she was one of the larger ships in the Great Lakes at the time.

On May 7, 1965, the Cedarville left Calcite, Michigan at around 5:00 am with a crew of 35. She was headed for Gary, Indiana with a payload of limestone when disaster struck. That morning a heavy fog surrounded the straits as the Cedarville approached. The only way the crew knew where they were and what surrounded them was through the ship's radar.

Soon after the Cedarville entered the Mackinac Straits, the Weissenberg appeared on its radar screen. The two ships made radio contact with each other to keep aloft of their locations. The Weissenberg also notified the Cedarville that there was another ship headed in their direction somewhere out in front of them. This ship did not appear on the Cedarville's radar screen, nor did it answer to repeated attempts to make contact through radio or horn signals.

Sailing blindly in the path of the faceless ship, Captain Joppich slowed the Cedarville down and turned to get out of the route most ships take through the straits. Unfortunately, it was too late and a collision was now imminent. Ivan

Trafelet was on Cedarville's deck and said "we didn't see the other ship until it was practically in our side."

Just as the two ships were about to collide, the Cedarville made a sharp turn to avoid impact. This hasty move caused the mystery ship to hit the Cedarville mid-ship and tear a 20-foot gash in her side. The ship began taking on water fast. Captain Joppich sounded a MAYDAY and believed that he could save the ship by beaching it before it sank. As the Cedarville struggled to reach the shallow water, she began to roll over. Jim Leitzow recalls "we were just about to launch the lifeboats when the ship tilted." The crew was only able to free one lifeboat, and most had to jump into the icy 40 degree waters.

The crew of the Weissenberg heard the cries of the Cedarville's survivors coming from the water as they passed the site of the accident and sent out their lifeboats. A total of twenty seven Cedarville crewmembers were pulled out of the freezing waters that day.

The accident claimed the lives of two men pulled aboard lifeboats. The first was deck watchman Edmund H. Jungman, who had drowned before the rescue boats had arrived. Second was wheelsman Stanley Haske. He was taken to the hospital, but died from extreme exposure and shock.

Five of the eight missing bodies were located over the course of the next several days. They were Reinhold F. Radtke, William B. Asam, Arthur J. Fuhrman, F. Donald Lamp, and Wilbert W. Bredow. The three that remained missing were: Charles H. Cook, Hugo Wingo, and Eugene F. Jones. The remains of Charles H. Cook were found by a S.C.U.B.A. diver about one year later and the unidentifiable remains of another crewmember eleven years later in 1976. The body of the third missing person has never been found.

As for the unidentified ship that hit the Cedarville, it was a 400-foot Norwegian ship named Topdalsfjord. The

crew claimed that they searched for survivors for five hours
with no luck and continued on their way. Unfortunately,
there were no radio signals, no horns sounded, no sign they
were ever there other than the damaged and sinking
Cedarville.

The investigation which followed illustrated that not
only was the Topdalsfjord commonly in the Great Lakes
and familiar with procedure, but also had working radar
onboard. In fact, the second officer, who operated the radar,
reported that he spotted a ship one and a half miles away.
The Topdalsfjord's chief officer, Carl Fagerli, also reported
that he sounded the ship's foghorn. The truth of this tragic
accident will remain a mystery.

The only punishment that the investigators could give
the Topdalsfjord was a fine of $100.00. The ship's crew
were foreign, as was the ship, and therefore could not be
tried.

There have been two additional deaths on the
Cedarville since it sank. Due to the ships popularity as a dive
site, accidents have occurred. Over the past 40 or so years,
two divers have joined the death toll claimed by the
Cedarville.

Eber Ward

Built: 1888
Sank: April 9, 1909
Size: Length 213'
Width: 37'
Height: 22'
Cause of Shipwreck: Icebergs
Crew Lost: 5

Named after the lighthouse keeper of Bois Blanc Island from 1829 to 1842, the Eber Ward now sits near the bottom of the Mackinac Bridge under 138 feet of water, not far from the post of the man for which she was named.

On April 9, 1909, the Straits of Mackinac were frigid and icebergs littered the water. It was this day that the Eber Ward and her crew of fourteen met their fate. On the first trip of the year, the Eber Ward was on her way from Chicago to Port Huron, with a stop in Milwaukee for 55,000 bushels of corn.

As the ship entered the Straits of Mackinac, the ice was growing thick. It was possible to navigate through, but Captain LeMay wanted to make good time and instead tried to break through the ice. The Eber Ward was approaching the location where the Mackinac Bridge now stands, when the wood "began to twist and crackle beneath" as it was losing the battle with the ice.

The water entering the hull started slowly, then became faster and faster. Before the crew could do much the ship was going down. Within ten minutes, the Eber Ward was gone. Of the fourteen crewmembers onboard, five were trapped below deck and went down with the ship. The remaining crew was quickly rescued by a ship called the Bennington. In time, the crewmen who lost their lives were recovered, as was the cargo.

Today, the Eber Ward has become a popular dive site and the ship has claimed several divers' lives. As recent as 1999, a diver died while exploring the Eber Ward. His body was found at the bottom of the straits with an empty tank. How this tragedy happened is still a mystery.

Peshtigo

Built: 1863
Sank: June 26, 1878
Size: Length 161'
Cause of Shipwreck: Collision
Crew Lost: 2

The Peshtigo left the port in Erie, Pennsylvania bound for Chicago with a cargo of coal. At the same time, the St. Andrew was sailing from Chicago to Buffalo. As the sun set on June 25, 1878, the crews of the Peshtigo and St. Andrew were in store for a long and tragic night. The weather was fair, except for a fog that had begun to roll into the area around the straits. The hour had approached 1 o'clock in the morning and Captain Peter Lynch of the Peshtigo had put his second mate, John Boyle, at the helm; a decision he would later regret. The events that followed are an eyewitness account from a crewmember of the St. Andrew.

"The St. Andrew had her starboard tacks on board and was working nicely, with her sheets well aft, when the Peshtigo was discovered heading towards her, upon which the St. Andrew showed her torch. The Peshtigo when abreast of the St. Andrew sheared aport and struck her amidships, and cut her to the water's edge. In a moment, both crews were on deck intent on discovering the amount of damage done. It was evident at once that both vessels were sinking."

Captain Lynch of the Peshtigo reportedly told his second mate "John, you done a bad job." The Peshtigo began to sink fast and the bow went down first, forcing the stern to raise high above the water. The ship sank in under 9 minutes. The St. Andrew sank slower and the crew had time to escape safely.

The crewmen who were lost in this tragedy, both from the Peshtigo, are John Boyle, the one assumed responsible for the accident, and an unknown man from the Buffalo area. The two men went below deck to gather their clothing after the ships collided. John Boyle never came back and the other man was almost rescued before he drowned.

The masts of the Peshtigo were visible on the surface of the straits for some time. Eventually, the ship and its masts vanished. The whereabouts of the Peshtigo are a mystery. However, the St. Andrew is still lying in the straits and divers visit it from time to time.

Another fact of interest is that the Captain of the St. Andrew was Edward Fitzgerald, son of the famed Edmund Fitzgerald. Edmund owned the St. Andrew and later was immortalized on the ship bearing his name, the famous freighter that sank with all hands on board in Lake Superior.

California

Built: 1873
Sank: October 3, 1887
Size: Length 137'
Width: 24'
Height: 13'
Cause of Shipwreck: Severe Weather
Crew & Passengers Lost: 9

On October 2, 1887, the California left Chicago on a routine voyage to Montreal. The ship had a crew of twenty-one under the command of Captain John V. Trowell. She was loaded with corn and pork, as well as five passengers. The accounts of the California's journey were retold by one of its passengers, a Mrs. Cornellus Connerton, just after her rescue:

"Our first day out from Chicago was comparatively quiet, but gradually it got rougher. By Monday, the pitching of the boat was terrible. The dishes were swept from the tables and piled in a heap with chairs and sofas. We could not cook anything all day. I sat on a little settee, with my feet braced against the wall to keep from being thrown down."

"All day we pitched about in that way, until just before dark I went to the captain and asked him to put in to some island. Nevertheless, there was no chance to do this. As darkness came on, we all huddled together in the cabin. Outside I could hear the roar of the water and could see that the night was very black. There was neither star nor moon. No lights on the shore could be seen. It was only black all around."

"No one thought of going to bed. There we sat in the cabin. The men began putting on life preservers. My dear son brought me one and put it around me. But the engineer noticed that it was on wrong, so he took it off and bound it around me, with two lashings over the shoulders."

"There we sat waiting for death. I got on my knees and prayed. One of the sailors next to me said "Oh, if I had my life to live over again I would do differently."

"The captain came back and I asked him if there was any hope. He only told me the time it was just 1 o'clock in the morning and then hurried forward."

"I had my life preservers on about 15 minutes when there was a crash. If the city hall had fallen, it could not have been more terrible than the noise of that fearful wave. The captain had turned the boat on the shore and it had struck. Then the boat keeled over on her side."

"I saw my son clinging to a doorway. Then the great wave came sweeping everyone before it except one sailor and myself. The next wave took us. I caught him by the pant leg and clung on, and we went into the water together."

"It seemed an hour. The water was in my mouth. I was choking. Chairs and spars were about me. I grasped at everything. I went under. Then the life preserver brought me up. A big piece of the cabin came near me. I reached it and got partly on it. There was an hour more in the darkness."

"Perhaps I was conscious. I don't know. But at last I saw a boat with two men in it. They drew me in. I fell in the bottom of the boat. I was saved but my darling son was gone. That's all. I can't talk anymore. My head is beating so. That's all. He's gone."

The California sank on October 3, 1887 just after 1:00 am. The ship is believed to have hit a shallow reef causing the ship to keel over and the tremendous waves finished her off. Within a matter of minutes, the doomed ship broke apart and sank. There was no time for the lifeboats to be properly launched. Those who did manage to get into them had to cut the lines attached, or be pulled down with the ship.

After the survivors were rescued, it was learned that eight of the crew (all men) were the first to the lifeboats. These crewmembers did not stay to help the women or passengers off the sinking ship. One of the same crewmembers later stated that Captain Trowell abandoned his post and caused the accident. However, Mrs. Connerton and another woman believe that if not for the captain and several of the ship's engineers, who helped them in the last moments before the ship sank, they would not have survived.

As the California sank that dark night, she took with her nine souls. Along with Mrs. Connerton's son, Cornellus Connerton Jr., the casualties were another passenger named Minnie Mambrey, the purser George Foley, a passenger's maid Elia Poppa, two deckhands William Tuff and Xavier Dant, a fireman Harvey Smith, and two cabin boys Arthur Hazardy and Robert Grant. The California now rests in the Straits of Mackinac near St. Helena Island.

The Indian Drum

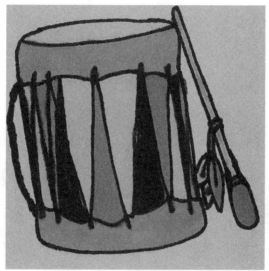

A sketch of a Native American drum.

Location:

The waters of the Great Lakes.

The Tale:

One of many Great Lakes legends is that of the Indian Drum (also known as the Ottawa Drum). This drum is said to sound one beat for every victim the waters of the Great Lakes has laid claim to.

The area in which the drum is most commonly heard is in and around the Straits of Mackinac. Unfortunately, the Indian Drum is rarely heard amongst Great Lakes tourists. Instead, it is more commonly heard by those of the Ottawa tribe and people whose lives are closely tied to the lakes.

The Drum's Haunting & Ghostly Activity Scale:

Time Scale: ★ ★

Intensity: ✳ ✳

Regularity: ✳

Spanning the Straits, The Mackinac Bridge

The Mackinac Bridge at sunset.

The Mackinac Bridge opened to the public in November of 1957, about 7 years ahead of schedule. Contrary to popular belief, there are no workers buried in the cement footings of the bridge. However, during construction, several accidents resulted in the deaths of five men.

The first death was that of Frank Pepper. Frank was a deep-water helmet diver and worked on submerged parts of the bridge. On September 10, 1954, he surfaced too fast and, as a result, died of the bends.

Second to die was James R. LeSarge. James lost his balance and fell into a 40-foot deep caisson, hitting his head on steel braces on the way down. His death occurred October 10, 1954.

Next was the death of Albert Abbott on October 25, 1954. Albert's death was the most unusual because he only fell 4 feet into the Straits of Mackinac and drowned. Several unsuccessful rescue attempts were made, but he died before being reached.

The last two deaths during the original construction process of the Mackinac Bridge were those of Jack C. Baker and Robert Koppen. The two men were working on the bridge towers high above the straits. On June 6, 1956, both Jack's and Robert's supports gave way under them, sending them tumbling over 400 feet into the straits below. Neither of the men survived and the body of Robert Koppen was never found.

Nearly 41 years later, one more bridge worker would join the original five. On August 7, 1997, Daniel Doyle of Sault Ste. Marie was part of a painting crew working on the bridge. He lost his balance and fell off his scaffold high above the straits. Daniel miraculously survived the fall but the water was a chilling 50 degrees and he soon went into shock and drowned.

Open for nearly half a century and accommodating over 100 million travelers, the bridge's passenger safety record is remarkable, especially considering the dangerous weather conditions that sometimes arise in the Mackinac Straits area. For example, on November 10, 1975 the bridge was closed due to 90 mile an hour winds (category one hurricane). That same day, about 70 miles away, the Edmund Fitzgerald went down with all 29 crewmembers.

However, things can and do happen which cannot be avoided. Since 1957, there have been several accidents on the bridge, some of which resulted in the fatalities. Nevertheless, no car had ever gone off the side of the bridge until 1989.

In September of 1989, a Royal Oak woman was driving her Yugo across the Mackinac Bridge. The presence of gale force winds caused her to lose control of her car. Witnesses say that the car swerved back and forth before hitting the side rail, when a gust of wind helped "lift" the tiny car enough for it to topple over the side of the bridge and plummet into the straits 199 feet below. The driver was believed to have survived the crash but drowned soon after the car hit the water.

The only other car to go over the side of the Mackinac Bridge was in March of 1997. On this occasion, the courts ruled it was not an accident, but a suicide. The victim, a man from Shelby Township, drove his Bronco at speeds around 60 to 65 miles per hour into the side rail. The truck launched off the bridge and crashed into the ice covered straits far below, ending the man's life.

The Shelby Township man was not the first to commit suicide on the Mackinac Bridge. Although not nearly as common an occurrence as on the Golden Gate Bridge in San Francisco, over the years, the bridge has attracted several unfortunate souls.

The exact number is a little difficult to say, but those people believed to have "jumped" off the Mackinac Bridge is seven or eight. This number accounts for those whose cars were found empty on the bridge with the person declared missing, those that someone witnessed jump, or times when a body was discovered in the Mackinac Straits near the bridge.

The first recorded "jumper" was a Royal Oak man in 1974. He parked his van near the middle of the bridge, stepped out and jumped. Since that first suicide, several more have followed occurring in 1985, 1987, 1996, 1997, 1998, and 2002. The most recent suicide was that of a Stockbridge woman who jumped off the bridge with her 6-month-old baby in her arms. Recently, rumors are surfacing that people crossing the bridge can occasionally hear the faint cries of a baby. Is this the ghost of the Stockbridge woman's baby?

As the Mackinac Bridge nears its 50th anniversary, perhaps the nearly 20 people who met their demise will join in the festivities with an unearthly appearance.

The Fatal Flight

The Towers of the Mackinac Bridge.

Tragic Tale:

On September 10, 1978, a small single engine Cessna, with three onboard, departed Camp Grayling, Michigan. They had planned an easy flight up to Mackinac Island.

The weather in the Straits of Mackinac that day was calm, which helped a thick blanket of fog to stay in place. This may account for the Cessna's crew becoming disoriented, flying blind as they reached the Mackinac Island area. The small plane was headed west through the straits near the Mackinac Bridge when tragedy struck.

Just after 12:00pm, the Cessna struck the 2 ½ inch steel suspension cables about 40 feet above the road on the eastern side of the Mackinac Bridge. The initial impact completely ripped off the wings of the small plane. The remaining body of the aircraft was able to clear the western cables and dove 200 feet into the waters below. Nobody traveling on the bridge was hurt and only a few pieces of the Cessna fell on the road below.

What was left of the airplane's body sank some 90 feet to the bottom of the Straits of Mackinac, with all passengers still onboard. A rescue effort was immediately put into action, but with cold waters and strong currents, divers surfaced empty-handed.

With no sign of survivors, the divers continued their search the next day. They eventually discovered what they feared; three lifeless bodies trapped in the wreckage at the bottom of the straits. Those men who joined the Mackinac Strait's growing list of dead were: Major Virgil Osborne, Captain James Robbins, and Captain Wayne Wisbrok. The men hailed from the St. Louis area and were in the Marine Corps Reserves.

MACKINAC ISLAND

A view of Mackinac Island from the straits.

Roughly 11,000 years ago, the prehistoric people of the Mackinac region looked out over the straits and saw a new island emerging from the water. The island had high bluffs and rose above the waters like the shell of a turtle. Thus, native people named it Mish-la-mack-in-naw, which loosely means "great turtle."

The island was awe-inspiring to those who first explored it. The early explorers believed that the island, with its magnificent natural rock formations, was a sacred place. Therefore, Mackinac Island was considered both a place of honor and a hallowed location to bury their dead.

Over time, the Island has not changed all that much. Most of the Island's natural wonders remain today, as do its mysteries. Many of those who live, work, or visit often, have tales of the Island's ghosts, legends, and tragic events.

Mackinac Island Locator Map

Mackinac Island Haunts & Legends

1. St. Anne's Cemetery
2. Original St. Anne's Cemetery
3. Mackinac Island Cemetery
4. Original Mackinac Island Cemetery
5. Post Cemetery
6. Battlefield of 1814
7. Skull Cave
8. Marquette Park
9. Grand Hotel
10. Hann's 1830 Inn
11. Fort Holmes
12. SugarLoaf
13. Rifle Range Trail
14. Arch Rock
15. Northern Woods
16. Crack In The Island
17. Devil's Lake (dry)
18. Lover's Leap
19. Devil's Kitchen
20. Stonecliffe Mansion
21. Frances Lacey Murder

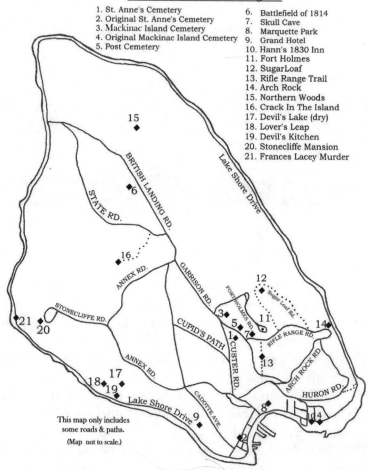

This map only includes
some roads & paths.

(Map not to scale.)

Island of The Dead

St. Anne's Cemetery Gates.

Mackinac Island was, and is, a huge cemetery. Throughout history, Mackinac Island has been used as burial grounds by one civilization or another.

The first people to come to the island were Native Americans who believed it to be the home of their god, Gitche Manitou (the Great Spirit). They proceeded to bury their dead on the Island for several hundred years. The exact locations of these burial grounds are not known, as many Native American cultures did not traditionally mark gravesites. However, some records, which existed prior to the early 1800's, indicated the gravesites of some American and British soldiers, civilians, and Native Americans buried on the Island. It is known that at least three cemeteries have been relocated and numerous Native American graves have been found during excavations.

The Known Cemeteries

St. Anne's Cemetery (ghost sightings)
Mackinac Island Map Location # 1 & 2

St. Anne's Cemetery on Mackinac Island was first established in 1779. It was located downtown, just off Hoban Street between Market and Main Street, next to the church of the same name (*refer to Downtown Map location #4, p.93*). The church building was moved to its present location on Main Street some time between 1820 and 1827, due in large part to the cemetery becoming overcrowded.

St. Anne's Cemetery, however, remained on Hoban Street until a suitable new location was found. Around 1852 a clearing in the woods off Garrison Road, not far from Fort Mackinac's Post Cemetery, was chosen as the location of the new St. Anne's Cemetery. The original cemetery, on Hoban Street, fell into disrepair and most of the graves were moved to the new location. The process of moving both the human remains and tombstones took over 30 years. In all that time, at least four graves were never moved to the new cemetery, just the tombstones.

The bodies that are believed to have remained buried at the Hoban Street location of St. Anne's Cemetery are Joseph Gleason, Abigail Legate, Elizabeth Mitchell, and Mary Putoff. Today, the Village Inn restaurant is situated where St. Anne's Church once stood and it is likely that human remains lie somewhere nearby or possibly beneath this building (*see Village Inn, p.101*).

Today, St. Anne's Cemetery sits quietly in the woods near Mackinac Island Cemetery and the Fort's Post Cemetery. The cemetery is still in use and available for those who qualify. However, in order to be buried in this cemetery, a person must be born on the Island or own property on the Island.

Ghostly Activity:

There are reports of a ghostly woman in a blue dress roaming the cemetery. However, her identity has remained a mystery.

St. Anne's Cemetery Haunting & Ghostly Activity Scale:
Time Scale: ★ ★ ★
Intensity: ✳ ✳ ✳
Regularity: ✳ ✳

Mackinac Island Cemetery
Mackinac Island Map Location # 3 & 4

The Mackinac Island Cemetery was once located next to the Mission Church on Main Street. Eventually, the cemetery was left abandoned and unused. In 1856, it was moved to its new location on Garrison Road. There is no record of human remains being left behind at the original Mackinac Island Cemetery, but no one knows for sure.

Today, Mackinac Island Cemetery sits near St. Anne's Cemetery and the Fort's Post Cemetery. This cemetery is also still in use and available for those who meet the same burial requirements as St. Anne's.

Fort Mackinac's Post Cemetery (ghost sightings)
Mackinac Island Map Location # 5

The Post Cemetery, one of only three military cemeteries where the flag permanently flies at half-staff, has been in use at its current location since the mid 1820's. The cemetery is located near both St. Anne's and Mackinac Island Cemeteries on Garrison Road. However, this is not the first cemetery used by Fort Mackinac. The first Post

Cemetery location is unknown due to poor record keeping, but is believed to be located behind Fort Mackinac, as several sets of human remains were unearthed there.

Ghostly Activity:
(see The Woman Who Weeps, p.57)

Fort Mackinac's Post Cemetery.

The Known Burial Grounds

The Battlefield of 1814 (ghost sightings)
Mackinac Island Map Location # 6

On August 4, 1814, the American forces fought the British in an attempt to regain control of Fort Mackinac. A bulk of the battle took place on and around what is now Wawashkamo Golf Course. During the course of the battle, 51 men were wounded and Major Andrew Hunter Holmes (for whom Fort Holmes is so named) was killed along with 12 of his fellow soldiers. The number of British soldiers who died in the battle is unknown. Those who died during the battle were later buried by the British commander Lieutenant Colonel Robert McDouall. The commander had the dead buried on the battlefield. Some have said the human remains were moved to the Post Cemetery, but there is no record of this ever happening. Those who died that day are almost certainly still buried beneath the Battlefield of 1814.

Ghostly Activity:

There have been reports of ghostly soldiers in the area. However, there are no known details of the encounters.

Battlefield of 1814's Haunting & Ghostly Activity Scale:

Time Scale: ★ ★ ★
Intensity: ✳ ✳ ✳
Regularity: ✳

Skull Cave

Mackinac Island Map Location # 7

This was the location of an ancient Native American burial ground. The bones for which the cave was named after have been removed from the site. *(see Skull Cave, p.59)*

Marquette Park

Mackinac Island Map Location # 8

This area in front of Fort Mackinac was once the location of a large Native American cemetery. As the story goes, a group of soldiers stationed at Fort Mackinac were digging up the soil in order to plant a garden. As they dug, they began to unearth human and animal remains. In all, the story claims that over 1,000 skeletons were found in Marquette Park.

Grand Hotel (ghost sightings)
Mackinac Island Map Location # 9

The grounds of Grand Hotel were also once the location of a Native American burial ground. As the foundation was laid, during the construction of the hotel, the workers found numerous human and animal remains buried throughout the build site.

Ghostly Activity:
(see Grand Hotel, p.94)

Haan's 1830 Inn
Mackinac Island Map Location # 10

During a construction project on the foundation in 1976, workers found remains of a Native American girl. She was buried just a few feet under the floor. It is believed the girl died around 1800.

Other Locations
These previous locations are the only known areas in which cemeteries and burial grounds exist. There are likely many other locations on Mackinac Island which hold the remains of Native Americans and maybe even some soldiers which have not yet been discovered. In fact, many people believe that if there is soil deep enough to bury someone, then someone is buried there already.

The Woman Who Weeps

The location in the Post Cemetery where the woman weeps.

Location:
>   At the rear corner of the Post Cemetery.
>   Mackinac Island Map Location # 5

Brief History:

The Post Cemetery holds the remains of several Fort Mackinac soldiers and their families. Family members buried at the Post Cemetery include two children of Lieutenant Calvin D. Cowles.

At the rear of the cemetery, on the left hand side, are the graves of Josiah Hamilton Cowles and his sister Isabel Hitchcock Cowles. Both died at a young age while their father was stationed at Fort Mackinac. Josiah was only 5 months old when he passed away in 1884 from a gastrointestinal disease. Four years later Isabel joined him, five weeks after she celebrated her first birthday in 1888.

The family grieved the tragic loss of their children. Mary, the children's mother and wife of Calvin, took the loss hardest. In her lifetime she lost three children to disease. She pained over her children's deaths and sorrow overcame her.

Ghostly Activity:

Although the task of identifying a ghost is difficult, the ghost that has been seen weeping over the graves of Josiah and Isabel is likely their sorrowful mother, Mary. The ghost has been described as a woman in a gown or long dress kneeling over the children's graves. She has a hazy appearance and disappears if approached. In a related ghost story, Mary's two children are believed to haunt the Officers' Hill Quarters at Fort Mackinac where the children lived with their parents.
(*see Fort Mackinac, p.110*)

Weeping Woman's Haunting & Ghostly Activity Scale:
Time Scale: ★ ★ ★
Intensity: ✷ ✷ ✷
Regularity: ✷ ✷

Skull Cave

The opening of Skull Cave.

Location:

> Near the corner of Garrison Road and Rifle Range
> Road.
> Mackinac Island Map Location # 7

Brief History:

Over 1,000 years ago, through the action of waves
against the shoreline, Skull Cave was formed. The location's
best known historical tale is that of Alexander Henry and
how he escaped with his life from local Native Americans.

After a Native American uprising at Fort
Michilimackinac on the mainland, Alexander Henry
escaped with the help of a Native American friend who
provided him safe passage to Mackinac Island. While
Alexander was on the Island, his friend warned him that "the
natives would be restless" and he would need to hide until
the danger passed.

As Alexander and his friend arrived at the opening of the cave, night was upon them. Alexander entered the cave and tried to get some sleep. After a difficult and uncomfortable night's sleep, the morning light revealed that the cave floor was covered in the skeletal remains of human bodies. What Alexander thought were sticks and rocks were actually human bones and skulls. After two days, Alexander's friend came back to give him the news that it was safe for him to return. From that day on, the cave has been called Skull Cave.

Legendary Tale:

There once was a chief named Ke-nu who was a maker of peace pipes. He was a great warrior and leader. However, his tribe had suffered many losses in war and as a result, his tribe had only a few braves left. The women which were in Ke-nu's tribe constantly conflicted over who should be able to marry these braves. Ke-nu grew tired of the fighting and set out to create peace pipes in which to settle the disputes.

Ke-nu took red clay to Skull Cave burial ground where he could make his peace pipes in complete silence. Once he was at the entrance of the cave, a skull rolled out in front of him. The skull then told Ke-nu to dig up the ground beneath his feet and he would find copper. With this copper, he was to make musical pipes or flutes. After the musical pipes were completed, he encased them in the red clay he brought. After the clay had dried, Ke-nu attached the pipe bowls to the ends of the pipes.

The skeletons in Skull Cave began to test the peace pipes Ke-nu had made. Suddenly, the skeletons became living men again. The men from Skull Cave returned with Ke-nu to his tribe and married all the bickering women. Once again Ke-nu was happy; now that his tribe was at peace once more.

Fort Holmes & Che-To-Wait's Ghost

Fort Holmes.

Location:

> *At the end of Fort Holmes Road, high above the rest of the Island.*
> *Mackinac Island Map Location # 11*

Brief History:

The highest point on the Island, at 320 feet above the lake, seems the likely place for a fort, or lookout, as so used by Native Americans for many generations. In 1812, the British Army built what was then named Fort George at this location. The Fort was small in size, but able to hold off American forces in 1814 and was never captured.   On February 18, 1815, The Treaty of Ghent gave Fort George and Mackinac Island to the United States. Fort George was later renamed Fort Holmes after Major Holmes (*see Fort Mackinac, p. 110*).

Legendary Tale:

Long ago, Che-to-wait and Mecostewanda, Native Americans, lived as husband and wife with their four sons in the Mackinac region. One day Che-to-wait, a great warrior, went away on a warpath and never returned. Nevertheless, Mecostewanda refused to accept that her beloved had passed to the realm of the dead, because she had not yet seen his ghost departing, as had other wives of warriors. So Mecostewanda sent her four sons out to find their missing father. One son traveled to the north, one to the south, one to the east, and the last to the west. As time passed and one by one her sons returned, no news of Che-to-wait's whereabouts was given.

Mecostewanda would sit for hours every day, high atop the hill where Fort Holmes is now located, watching for her husband. One day as the sun began to set over the Straits of Mackinac, she spotted a small boat made of rock and stone with sails of feathers. The pilot of the craft was the ghost of Che-to-wait. He was singing a ceremonial song the dead sing as they depart the world of the living. Finally, Mecostewanda could come to terms with the death of her husband.

Today, Fort Holmes is still a place many go for wonderful views of Mackinac Island and the lake below. Perhaps you may even see the ghost of Che-to-wait or Mecostewanda sailing away to realm of the dead.

Fort Holmes' Haunting & Ghostly Activity Scale:

Time Scale: ★

Intensity: ✱ ✱ ✱

Regularity: ✱

The Monolith Sugarloaf

Surrounded by dense woods, Sugarloaf stands tall.

Location:
> *Off Sugarloaf Road, below Point Lookout.*
> *Mackinac Island Map Location # 12*

Brief History:

Formed thousands of years ago, Sugarloaf was once a small island in the ancient Lake Algonquin, which covered most of the area. Records show that around 100 years ago the stone tower measured 90 feet and had some small trees growing on it. Today, the tower of brecciated limestone stands 15 feet lower at 75 feet with some small bushes. Time and the elements have eroded Sugarloaf an average of approximately 1.8 inches per year.

Legendary Tales:
There are three stories associated with Sugarloaf:

1.   A common Native American story about Sugarloaf claims that it was once home to a giant beehive. The bees of Sugarloaf lived in every crack and crevice and filled the towering rock with the finest honey. Many generations of Native people from the area would collect the sweet treat from the stone.

This story has been passed down for generations and it is possible, if not likely, that bees could have once lived in Sugarloaf. What happened to the bees? Nobody seems to know, but conditions do favor a safe and secure location for a beehive. Perhaps someday the bees will return.

2.   The second tale is about the Great Spirit or Git-chi Man-i-tou and his home away from home. Git-chi Man-i-tou would visit Mackinac Island before the time of man. When he stayed on the Island, he would take residence at Sugarloaf, his wigwam.

Upon reaching the Island, Git-chi Man-i-tou would come ashore at the location now home to Mission Point Resort. He would climb the Giant Staircase (formally located to the North of Mission Point) and pass through Arch Rock which were both on the way to his wigwam (Sugarloaf).

As the time of man approached, Git-chi Man-i-tou left Mackinac Island for the Northern Lights. He left behind his wigwam, which we now call Sugarloaf.

3.   This legend involves the great Native American named Man-a-boz-ho. Man-a-boz-ho, well known among his people for magical abilities, retired on Mackinac Island. During his lifetime, he was known as a messenger of Git-chi Man-i-tou (Great Spirit) and a powerful medicine man.

Ten braves, living south of Mackinac Island, grew up hearing tales of Man-a-boz-ho and his great magic. One day, the braves decided to find the great medicine man and ask him to grant their most desired wishes. For several months the braves traveled in search of Mackinac Island and Man-a-boz-ho, finally, reaching his home on the island.

The leader of the braves stepped forward and presented gifts of tobacco and wampum to Man-a-boz-ho. The leader asked if Man-a-boz-ho would perform a last act of magic and grant the braves' wishes. Man-a-boz-ho agreed.

All of the braves' wishes, but one, were comprised of skills common to man. Some of their wishes included becoming a great chief, hunter, or medicine man. The tenth and last brave approached Man-a-boz-ho and placed gifts on the ground in front of him. His wish was to live forever and never die. Man-a-boz-ho was very angry. All the other braves wished for gifts achievable to man. Yet the tenth brave asked for a power in which no man was to have. However, Man-a-boz-ho had agreed to grant all the braves' wishes, a promise he would keep.

The tenth brave began to twist, turn and grow taller and taller. His skin started to turn to stone and before long, he had become Sugarloaf. Forever to live as a pillar of solid rock.

Ghostly Activity:

Sightings have reported a number of small lights flying around Sugarloaf rock. The identity of these lights is a mystery.

Sugarloaf's Haunting & Ghostly Activity Scale:
    Time Scale: ★ ★ ★
    Intensity: ✷ ✷
    Regularity: ✷

The Ghostly Soldier of Rifle Range Trail

A view down Rifle Range Trail

Location:

Located directly behind Fort Mackinac.
Mackinac Island Map Location # 13 or refer to
Downtown Map location # 11

Brief History:

Rifle Range Trail is a narrow dirt path lined on either side by grass and trees. The trail gradually slopes down from Fort Holmes to Fort Mackinac's rear entrance. As the name implies, the trail was once used by Fort soldiers for target practice. The layout of the rifle range and its multilevel design is still seen today. However, this lonely path may have a troublesome past. It may be the site of Mackinac Island's first execution.

A Tale of Two Soldiers

On December 5, 1828, two soldiers stationed at Fort Mackinac, Corporal Hugh Flinn and Private James Brown, had an argument. During the disagreement, Brown stated to Flinn "God knows which one of us will live the longest!" The argument ended and nothing was thought of it.

Later that afternoon, Private Brown borrowed a musket rifle from one of the Fort officers for duty the next day. He took the musket to the mess hall where several soldiers, including Corporal Flinn, were relaxing after a hard days work. A gunshot abruptly sounded and Corporal Flinn collapsed, blood spewing from his neck. Brown held the smoking gun. As Flinn lay dying, Brown shouted, "My God! What have I done?" Pleading that it was an accident, but with no one witnessing the actual shot, Brown was arrested and charged with murder.

A gun similar to the one used by Private Brown.

Private Brown would spend the next 14 months fighting for his innocence in the courts. If he lost his case in one court, he appealed for a new trial in another. Eventually he was sentenced to "hang by the neck until dead." Brown awaited his punishment on Mackinac Island.

During Brown's imprisonment on Mackinac Island, he befriended Reverend William M. Ferry of the Mission Church and School. Reverend Ferry attempted to "save the soul" of Private Brown by converting him to Christianity.

However, Brown would not convert. He believed he would, "meet death like a hero, not like a coward."

Mrs. Ferry, Reverend Ferry's wife, circulated a petition, which was sent to The President of The United States, Andrew Jackson, to help pardon Private Brown of his sentence. She claimed that many people believed the man was innocent of the crime and the shooting was just an accident. Private Brown's legal counsel also made an attempt for a pardon from both Michigan's Governor Cass and President Andrew Jackson.

On December 25, 1829, six fellow soldiers and friends of Private Brown made a failed attempt at a mutiny of Fort Mackinac. They, too, believed Brown was innocent and wanted to free him before his execution. The six involved attacked a superior officer, Lieutenant Ephraim K. Smith, but were arrested and imprisoned at the Fort's guardhouse.

No pardons ever came to the condemned Private Brown. On Monday, February 1, 1830, Private James Brown's sentence was carried out and he was, "hung by the neck until dead." Gallows for the occasion were constructed especially for the execution, as Brown was the first person ever to be executed on Mackinac Island. The location in which the execution took place is unknown. However, it was likely a location near Fort Mackinac. Perhaps it happened at the Rifle Range.

The execution of Private Brown was one of the many cases which caused the State of Michigan to abolish capital punishment. People feared that an innocent person could be found guilty and executed.

Ghostly Activity:
This trail has a reputation of phantom bullets hissing past tourists' and locals' ears. Several people have even felt

as if someone, or something, was following them down the path.

However, the most conclusive sighting on record is from a state employee. One day during the summer as the sun was setting, a state employee and his fiancée were walking down from Fort Holmes. About half way to Fort Mackinac, he felt as if someone had stepped on the back of his shoe. When he turned to see who it was, a soldier in full uniform was standing in front of them and then quickly vanished. Who is this phantom soldier?

Perhaps it is the ghost of Private James Brown, executed so many years ago. The location of his execution is unknown and he just may be trying to make one last plea for his innocence. So take a stroll down Rifle Range Trail and see if this ghost pays you a visit.

Rifle Range Trail's Haunting & Ghostly Activity Scale:
Time Scale: ★ ★ ★
Intensity: ✹ ✹ ✹
Regularity: ✸ ✸ ✸

Arch Rock

Arch Rock sitting high above the lake.

Location:

> *Off Lakeshore Road on the East side of the Island,*
> *not too far past Robinson's Folly.*
> *Mackinac Island Map Location # 14*

Brief History:

One of Mackinac Island's best known natural formations, Arch Rock, sits approximately 150 feet above

Lake Shore Drive. This limestone formation is the result of the lake's constant wave action breaking down softer rock over a long period. As the water levels dropped, more of Arch Rock was exposed giving us the natural wonder seen today.

     A secondary arch, called Maiden Arch, can be seen at the base of Arch Rock (only visible from Lake Shore Drive).

Maiden Arch.

Legendary Tales:

     There is more than one Native American legend about Arch Rock. The three most popular tales are detailed here.

1.   There was a chief of the Ottawa Nation who angered the "Master of Life." As punishment, the "Master of Life" created winds so strong that they not only shook the earth and skies above, but stopped the midday sun. As the sun was accustomed to setting at the end of the day, it promptly fell

from the sky and crashed into the earth at the location now known as Arch Rock. This impact left behind a hole in the earth seen today. The next day the "Master of Life" had controlled his anger and the winds returned to normal. From that day forward, the sun set as it always had before.

2.   Arch Rock was Mackinac Island's gateway for the Great Manitou when he would visit. Upon arrival to the Island, the Great Manitou would dock his canoe at the two giant boulders found at the base of Arch Rock. He would then climb the Giant Staircase (which no longer exists) and pass through Arch Rock on his way to Sugarloaf, his wigwam home on the Island.

3.   There was once a woman named Ne-Daw-Niss (She-who-walks-like-the-mist). She was the daughter of a widowed Chippewa Chief. Ne-Daw-Niss worked hard and did both her chores and those of her departed mother. The Chief was proud of his daughter and knew she would make someone a fine wife.

    At her father's urging, Ne-Daw-Niss greeted many suitors, but found none to her liking. In time, Ne-Daw-Niss grew sad and withdrawn. The Chief was concerned and asked her what was wrong. She explained that she had met a man with whom she fell in love. Her father was happy, but could not understand why his daughter was so sad. Ne-Daw-Niss told her father that he was a Sky person she met one night while collecting rice in her canoe. He was greatly angered by this news because the marriage of a human and a Sky person was forbidden.

    Ne-Daw-Niss's father took her to the Island of The Great Turtle (Mackinac Island) and bound her hands and feet. He placed her atop a stone cliff and told her she could not return until she agreed to marry a human brave. There Ne-Daw-Niss sat, weeping night and day, refusing to abandon the love she had for the Sky person. Over time, her tears washed away the hard rock beneath her, forming Arch Rock. Afterwards, Ne-Daw-Niss was reunited with her one true love who brought her to his home in the sky.

The Massacred Native Ghosts

A clearing in the woods on the northern end of the Island.

Location:
> *Throughout the woods on the northern portion of the Island.*
> *Mackinac Island Map Location # 15*

Brief History:
> The northern part of Mackinac Island is the least explored by tourists, especially at night. It is here on the Island that the British are rumored to have murdered 70 or

more Native Americans. The story claims that the Natives were hunted by the British soldiers and killed throughout the woods north of the Island airport.

Ghostly Activity:

Some of the residents of Mackinac Island report seeing the ghostly images of Native American men running through the woods in the northern reaches of the Island. Tourists brave enough to venture into the dark woods have also claimed to see ghosts of men covered in blood escaping from an unseen enemy. Occasionally, their voices can also be heard in the winds that blow through the trees.

Natives' Haunting & Ghostly Activity Scale:
Time Scale: ★ ★
Intensity: ✱ ✱ ✱
Regularity: ✱

The Giant In The Crack-in-the-Island

Location:

On Crack-in-the-Island Trail, just north of the Island airport.
Mackinac Island Map Location # 16

Brief History:

The Crack-in-the-Island formed thousands of years ago. As water ran through the rock, it cut a deep crevice into the ground. The depth of the opening at one time was so deep that tourists brought rudimentary climbing gear in an attempt to descend to the floor of the crack. Over the years, the depth of the crack has lessened. Dirt, leaves, and other debris have since filled the deep fissure. Today, the opening is shallow enough to see the bottom.

View down into The Crack-in-the-Island.

Legendary Tale:

The area surrounding the Crack-in-the-Island has been known as dark and mysterious ever since Native Americans visited the Island. Early trappers, hunters, and

Natives would not even eat game which was caught in this "evil" place. Those brave or foolish enough to attempt entering the depths of the crack are said to have never returned.

The legend behind these superstitions comes from a Native tale of the giants that once lived on Mackinac Island. The story explains how at the beginning of time, giants ruled the Island and when the time of man came, they were commanded by the Great Spirit (Git-chi Man-i-tou) to leave the earth. Some of the giants became boulders, while others with evil hearts became unfeeling and cruel men.

One of the giants refused to become a pitiful rock or lowly human, believing he was too majestic to simply bow down and surrender to the time of man. Therefore, he tried to escape the will of the Great Spirit and retreated to the underworld. Here he could live where the spirits of the dead dwelled.

In order for the treasonous giant to reach the underworld, it was necessary to descend deep into the Crack-in-the-Island. As the giant began climbing down the crevice, his hands stuck to the opening. He tried to free himself, but with no success; the giant was trapped.

Unknown to the evil giant, the Great Spirit learned of his plan to escape and trapped him as punishment for his disobedience. After the giant was trapped, he was turned to stone; forever to remain in the Crack-in-the-Island.

The legend also states that those who walk upon the stone fingers of the giant will be cursed. Misfortunes such as blindness, bad luck, and loss of wealth are said to follow those who do. Although the fingers are difficult to see, the superstitious should use caution near the edge of the crack.

The Devil In The Lake

Location:
> *Part of the residential area now known as Hubbard's Annex off Annex Road.*
> *Mackinac Island Map Location # 17*

Brief History:
> In an area high above Devils' Kitchen, which is now a location for summer cottages called Hubbard's Annex, an ancient lake once existed. This body of water, which has since dried up, was named Devil's Lake.

Legendary Tale:
> Native American legend has it that Devil's Lake was a bottomless lake and home to a hideous and evil creature known as the evil Manitou or Geebis.
> The Geebis has been described as having the limbs, hands, head, and face of a human but with horns like a bull on its head. Its body is like that of an Ox, with cloven hoofs for feet. It is also commonly surrounded by an eerie blue glow. Several stories describe this creature's insatiable hunger for human flesh.
> It is the Geebis's hunger which explains why Devil's Lake was once the site of a horrible, but legendary Native American tradition. An ancient tradition stated that if a child was born with physical deformities, they were an incarnation of God's anger and must be destroyed. Devil's Lake was the place these children were thrown. It was believed that once drowned in the dark waters, the bodies would never be seen again, perhaps because the Geebis ate them.
> Another legend of Devil's Lake involves a young Native American couple. The wife of Little Rail, unfamiliar with Mackinac Island, came upon a pool of "musical waters" one beautiful day. She decided to bathe in the calm cold

waters, unaware of the evil spirits hidden deep below the surface.

As she entered the lake, storm clouds suddenly appeared and the winds began to scream through the trees. As the "musical waters" began howling, all the animals ran for cover. She knew that something was terribly wrong. Her instinct to flee was halted when a flash of lightning revealed a shape in the lake moving toward her at tremendous speed. The woman, paralyzed by an unknown force, witnessed the beast surfacing from the waters in front of her. The beast was the evil Geebis, an evil Manitou, or spirit, that lived in the lake.

The horrible devil grabbed hold of the fair maiden and tore the clothing from her. The beast proclaimed that she was now to forever remain in its service. Under a spell and trapped in a body she could no longer control, she was powerless to the Geebis' commands.

Adding to her troubles, she could see her husband, Little Rail, coming towards them, but was unable to warn him. Little Rail saw the beast holding his wife and charged in to save her. He fought the creature with all the strength he possessed, but it was no use; the beast was just too powerful. Exhausted, Little Rail sat upon the edge of the lake and watched the beast manipulate his dear wife's body like a puppet.

The Geebis made Little Rail's wife dance for him. Her beauty was intoxicating to the creature. The Geebis told Little Rail that he would take his bride to his home at the bottom of the lake for the rest of her days. Little Rail begged for her release, but the beast would not listen. The creature said that the two lovers would only be reunited when the bottomless lake became dry land. Only then would his wife be returned to him. As Little Rail sat weeping at the lake's edge, the Geebis grabbed hold of him and broke his back.

The rest of Little Rail's days would now be spent as a hunchback.

Little Rail spent the following days throwing stones into the lake, hoping that one day the lake would fill and he would be reunited with his love. It soon became a custom for Natives in the area to throw rocks in the lake to gain penance for their wrongdoings. They would also throw in an extra rock to help speed the reunion of the two lovers.

Over the years that followed, the evil Manitou in the lake could be heard laughing at Little Rail and the tragedy he had created. As time passed, however, the Geebis' laughter was silenced. Devil's Lake was finally filled by the pebbles and rocks thrown into its dark waters and the lovers were reunited.

Although Devil's Lake dried up long ago, and the laughter of the evil Geebis has been silenced, waters from the lake still flow from deep inside the Island near Devil's Kitchen. If you look northwest of Devil's Kitchen just a few feet, you can spot the stream flowing out of a small cave in the rock near the road.

Lover's Leap

Location:

Off Lakeshore Road above and to the northwest of Devil's Kitchen.
Mackinac Island Map Location # 18

Towering above the Straits of Mackinac sits a 145-foot limestone formation named Lover's Leap. Unfortunately, this formation hides behind many trees and bushes, making it difficult, if not impossible, to see from the shore below. Furthermore, this giant landmark is currently on private property and accessible only to those with permission.

Legendary Tale:

The legend of Lover's Leap involves two lovers who were forbidden to see each other. Ge-niw-e-gwon and Michinimockonong were in love and wanted to marry. Michinimockonong's father, a great chief named Shot-a-way-way, felt that the man who had captured his daughter's heart was socially inferior.

Shot-a-way-way demanded that if the young brave wished to marry his daughter, he must prove himself worthy of her. Therefore, Shot-a-way-way gave Ge-niw-e-gwon a list of tasks to complete in order to win his daughter's hand. The tasks were much too difficult for an inexperienced brave and included the scalping of a powerful enemy named Saugatuk and the theft of his war-horse.

Regardless of whether Ge-niw-e-gwon succeeded, Shot-a-way-way, nonetheless, arranged for him to be murdered, since he would never allow his daughter to marry such a lowly man. Consequently, the murderer would take Ge-niw-e-qwon's place as Michinimockonong's husband at the request of Shot-a-way-way.

Michinimockonong agreed with Ge-niw-e-gwon that she would wait for his return at their favorite meeting place (the top of Lover's Leap). Each day that her love was away, she would sit dressed in her bridal outfit atop the rocky cliff waiting patiently for his return. As Michinimockonong waited, she listened to the birds singing and heard them tell the story of Ge-niw-e-gwon's victory in battle, while another bird sang of treachery and betrayal on the part of her father. It was then that she learned of Shot-a-way-way's plan to wed her to Mutch-i-ki-wish after he murdered Ge-niw-e-gwon.

When news of Ge-niw-e-gwon's approach finally reached Michinimockonong, she rushed to the edge of the lover's cliff to catch sight of him. To her horror, the canoe contained the motionless body of her lover. The pilot of the canoe was Mutch-i-ki-wish. He had carried out her father's wishes and murdered Ge-niw-e-gwon. Now he was coming for payment; Michinimochonong's hand in marriage.

Enraged by the sight of her beloved's body, she took aim with her bow and fired a fatal shot through the heart of Mutch-i-ki-wish. His body fell into the water and was never seen again.

As Ge-niw-e-gwon's body floated nearer, Michinimockonong declared to those around her, "He waits for me! Tell my father I will not come. Tell him that Git-chi-Man-i-tou hath said: "Every man of Shot-a-way-way's line shall die by fire. Shot-a-way-way, his sons, and his son's sons shall burn to death in the lodge of the women they love!" She then leaped off the towering cliff to join her beloved in the waters of the lake below. The lovers were once again reunited and swam off to become the mother and father of all fish.

Ghostly Activity:

There are rumors that the ghost of Michinimockonong can still be seen jumping from the top of Lover's Leap to join her Ge-niw-e-gwon in the afterlife. However, the actual pillar of rock is concealed by trees and bushes and difficult to see from below. In recent years, sightings of Michinimockonong's ghost have not been common and the only way to easily see the rock pillar is from the top, which is private property.

Lover's Leap Haunting & Ghostly Activity Scale:
Time Scale: ★
Intensity: ★★★
Regularity: ✳

The Devil's Kitchen

Is this the place where men were cooked, alive!?

Location:

> On the West side of the Island, just off Lakeshore
> Road.
> Mackinac Island Map Location # 19

Brief History:

Devil's Kitchen is also known as the Cave of The
Red Geebis. The "kitchen" was used by some people
throughout history as a shelter because a fire could burn
there during inclement weather. These fires have charred
the rock and may be the basis for the legend that surrounds
this place.

Legendary Tale:

Two very similar stories exist about Devil's Kitchen. In fact, the two stories are the same except for a few minor details.

As summer ended and fall approached, the tribes on Mackinac Island would begin preparing their move to the mainland for the winter. Aikie-wai-sie was now an old man and could no longer travel with his tribe. He decided to stay behind and end his days on Mackinac Island.

Aikie-wai-sie's granddaughter, Willow-Wand, either stayed behind to care for her grandfather or was left behind by accident. She soon realized that the two of them were in danger since there was not enough food to last the winter. Willow-Wand hung either a white deerskin with markings on it or a large red blanket high upon a cliff, hoping it would attract local fishermen near the Island and give them rescue. Willow-Wand especially hoped her beloved Kewe-naw would either find or rescue her.

Kewe-naw, who had declared his love for Willow-Wand, had left the Island before knowing of her intention to remain. Willow-Wand knew that if he learned of her circumstances, he would surely come to their aid.

While awaiting a rescue, Willow-Wand and her grandfather remained high above Devil's Kitchen in the cave of a black bear. Night after night, the food supply shrank and screams of men being cooked alive for the Red Geebis' feasts filled the air. The Red Geebis was a devilish creature similar to the Geebis in Devil's Lake (see *The Devil In The Lake, p.78*). As time passed, Willow-Wand and Aikie-wai-sie's food ran out, as did their water. Although the lake was right below them, it was far too dangerous to collect its water with demons still present.

Unknown to Willow-Wand, she possessed the power to unleash water from both ground and rocks at her command. However, this power would only come to her after she fasted for seven days. Aikie-wai-sie watched on as his granddaughter suffered, powerless to help ease her torment.

On the seventh day, Willow-Wand could endure no more. Her thirst had to be quenched. She picked up a rock and screamed "water" while smashing it into the wall of the cave. A stream of water suddenly began to flow from the side of the cave. The two drank until they could drink no more.

As the cries of the men burning below grew louder and louder, Willow-Wand looked down toward Devil's Kitchen. To her horror, she discovered that Kewe-naw, who had come to rescue her, was now a prisoner of the Red Geebis. Bound and unable to escape, Kewe-naw awaited his turn to be cooked alive over the demon's fires.

Taking full advantage of her newly discovered powers, Willow-Wand quickly released a flood of water from the ground to extinguish the demon's fire. She then sent a rainbow bridge for Kewe-naw to climb. As soon as he reached her, Willow-Wand released a deluge upon the Red Geebis and the devils below were drowned.

Now finally safe, Willow-Wand, her grandfather, and Kewe-naw decided to remain on the Island. With the hunting skills of Kewe-naw and the firewood left by the Red Geebis, the three lived comfortably in the cave of the black bear until the tribe returned in the spring.

Stonecliffe Mansion

A view of the front of Stonecliffe Mansion

Location:

> *8593 Cudahy Circle*
> *At the end of Stonecliffe Road, near the Woods*
> *Restaurant.*
> *Mackinac Island Map Location # 20*

Brief History:

Michael Cudahy was a businessman who ran a successful packaged meat company and made profitable real estate investments. In 1904, he purchased 150 acres on Mackinac, making him the Island's largest landowner at the time. With the aid of architect Fredrick Perkins, (who also designed the Governor's Cottage on the Island) Stonecliffe Mansion was built that same year.

Michael, his wife, and their 7 children enjoyed Stonecliffe together for the next five years. Then, in 1910, Michael passed away leaving the property to his family.

In 1915 the Cudahy family sold Stonecliffe to Alvin (*aka. Tobe*) and Sallie Hert. The Herts added a playhouse on the property for their children. This building is currently the home of The Woods restaurant.

Unfortunately, Mr. Hert died six years after purchasing Stonecliffe. His wife Sallie continued to use the property until her own death in 1948. The Mansion was then left to the Episcopal Cathedral Foundation of Washington.

The Episcopal Cathedral Foundation of Washington retained possession of Stonecliffe Mansion and the surrounding property until 1966 when the property was sold to the Moral Re-Armament Movement (M.R.A.).

The Moral Re-Armament group's purpose is defined as "the good road of an ideology inspired by God upon which all can unite. Catholic, Jew or Protestant, Hindu, Muslim, Buddhist and Confucians - all find they can change, where needed, and travel along this good road together." Some believe this group was an early version of Alcoholics Anonymous (*see Mission Point, p. 140, for a more thorough description of the M.R.A.*).

The M.R.A. used the property as a retreat for high-level members. They also implemented many upgrades and additions during their ownership.

In 1972 the property was turned into a ski resort which operated until 1979. Since 1979, the property has changed owners several times. Currently, the Bacon family owns Stonecliffe. The Bacons have expanded the resort to accommodate more people and greatly improved its amenities. Stonecliffe Resort is truly a place where you can get away from the grind and unwind, as it is located in a tranquil forest setting far from the noise and crowds of downtown.

Ghostly Activity:

The ghost that is believed to haunt the Stonecliffe Mansion has been a resident of the estate almost since it was built. She was a servant girl who worked for the Cudahy family. It is unknown why, but she committed suicide somewhere in the apple orchards that once grew throughout the Stonecliffe property.

The girl's ghost is usually found in her former quarters on the third floor of the original Stonecliffe mansion. The servant girl's room is now called "Maplewood" and the scent of apples is the most common experience visitors report. However, some have claimed to have had furniture in this room unexplainably moved around, even blocking the door from time to time making entry to the room difficult. On rare occasions, some have even seen her ghost and one person even captured a photograph of the apparition.

Recently, the ghostly servant girl appeared to a small group of tourists on their way back to Stonecliffe. The group was riding in a taxi late one summer night when the ghost appeared directly in the path of the carriage. The horses spooked and the taxi stopped. The passengers all ran from the taxi and the driver managed to turn the carriage around, quickly departing. The driver was said to have quit the next day, leaving the Island never to return.

Even though the ghost has spooked a few horses, there is no need to be cautious around her. The ghost of the servant girl reportedly is a good-natured spirit and means no harm to anyone.

Stonecliffe's Haunting & Ghostly Activity Scale:
Time Scale: ★ ★ ★
Intensity: ✶ ✶ ✶
Regularity: ✳ ✳

The Murder of Frances Lacey

Location:

> In the area on Lake Shore Road near Sunset rock
> and Stonecliffe Resort.
> Mackinac Island Map Location # 21

Tragic Tale:

On July 24, 1960, the peace of Mackinac Island was tragically disrupted when a rapist and murderer visited. His victim was Frances Lacey, a middle-aged woman visiting from Dearborn, Michigan, with her daughter and son-in-law.

Frances Lacey's story begins at the Murray Hotel. She left the hotel around 9:00am on Sunday to make the three and a half mile walk to a cottage rented by her daughter and son-in-law near British Landing. She never arrived.

Mrs. Lacey's daughter, worried about her mother's unusual tardiness, contacted the Mackinac Island Police. The search that followed was the most intense the Island has ever seen. Over 60 residents of the Island, State Police, Boy Scouts, Bloodhounds, State Park employees, and the Coast Guard were involved in the massive search. Mrs. Sutter, Frances Lacey's daughter, said, "I'm going to stay on the Island as long as it takes to find her. I'll do it even if it takes two years to find her and I have to become a beachcomber in the process." Four days later at about 7:15pm, the lifeless body of Frances Lacey was found.

As the police pieced the events together, they came to one conclusion. The authorities believe that Mrs. Lacey was attacked at about 10:00am Sunday July 24th on Lake Shore Road. She had been struck in the head so hard that her dental plate was dislodged from her mouth. The attacker then dragged her about 20 feet into the woods and sexually assaulted her. After the assault, the suspect took Mrs. Lacey's underwear and used it to strangle her. Her body was hidden under some bushes and a fallen tree nearby.

The authorities could find no motive and the large crowds of tourists made finding the killer nearly impossible. There are theories as to who killed Frances Lacey, but still no proof. Some believe that the killer was a guest of the Moral Re-Armament (M.R.A.) group, who were using Stonecliffe Mansion at the time. Others say it was just some warped criminal loose on the Island. Regardless of who they were, the killer has gotten away with murder.

The Mischievous Dwarf Fairies

Location:
Found throughout the Island.

Brief History:
Mackinac Island is ever changing. Trees fall in the forest, rocks roll down hills, and people leave their mark. However, a Native American legend may explain why so many have found themselves lost on Mackinac Island.

Legendary Tale:

The story tells of small dwarf fairies or spirits that live in every tree, knoll, flower, and rock on the Island. The tribes of the area call them Putwujinnini or "little dancing people" and these fairies continue to be troublemakers to humans on Mackinac Island.

The Putwujinnini understand everything that nature has provided, only humans are a mystery to them. The legend describes how their only source of amusement is watching how people react when they are lost. People hiking, riding, or biking through the Island's interior may find, on their return route, that rocks, bushes, tree branches, and/or other small natural landmarks have been moved by the Putwujinnini. This can often cause confusion, leading a person to question where they are.

Losing one's bearings is not exclusive to those unfamiliar with the Island. Several long-time residents have found themselves suddenly "lost" while venturing from the Island's interior. So if you do become lost on Mackinac Island, remember two things. First, the Island is not large and you will find your way back to town eventually. Second, you might be the best entertainment for a supernatural creature, so do your best to put on a good show!

A view of downtown Mackinac Island from high above.

MACKINAC ISLAND DOWNTOWN

Mackinac Island's downtown is where you will find large crowds of tourists throughout the summer months. It is also where a majority of the Island's ghostly residents reside. They inhabit houses, bed and breakfasts, and hotels, amongst other places. Some of the ghosts have become fairly well known, while others are rarely mentioned. Both types of stories can be found in the following chapter.

93

Downtown Mackinac Locator Map

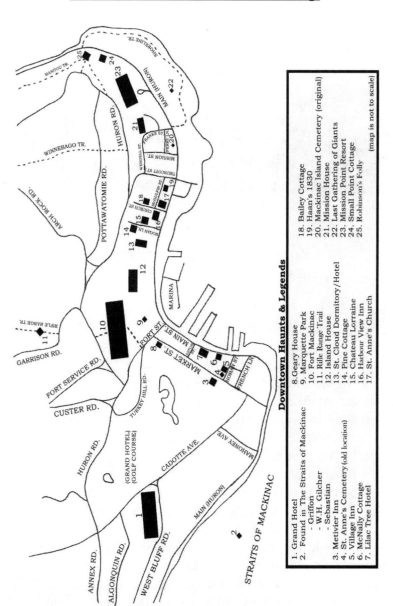

Downtown Haunts & Legends

1. Grand Hotel
2. Found in The Straits of Mackinac
   - Griffon
   - W.H. Gilcher
   - Sebastian
3. Metivier Inn
4. St. Anne's Cemetery (old location)
5. Village Inn
6. McNally Cottage
7. Lilac Tree Hotel
8. Geary House
9. Marquette Park
10. Fort Mackinac
11. Rifle Range Trail
12. Island House
13. St. Cloud Dormitory/Hotel
14. Pine Cottage
15. Chateau Lorraine
16. Harbour View Inn
17. St. Anne's Church
18. Bailey Cottage
19. Haan's 1830
20. Mackinac Island Cemetery (original)
21. Mission House
22. Last Gathering of Giants
23. Mission Point Resort
24. Small Point Cottage
25. Robinson's Folly

(map is not to scale)

Grand Hotel

The majestic Grand Hotel.

Location:

> *Found on the western edge of the Downtown area.*
> *Downtown Mackinac Map Location # 1*

Brief History:

Built in 1887 by Central Railroad, Indiana Railroad, and the Cleveland Steamship Navigation Company, Grand Hotel was designed to be the finest example of a summer resort in the world. Over the years, there have been several owners, expansions, and slight remodels, but the overall prestigious look and feel of the hotel has always remained.

Few hotels in existence today are able to lay claim to some of the honors held by Grand Hotel. Besides having the longest front porch in the world (660 feet), Grand Hotel is also the World's largest Summer resort. Furthermore, Grand Hotel has been host to many famous guests including five U.S. presidents (Truman, Kennedy, Ford, Clinton, and Bush), Mark Twain, and Thomas Edison. In fact, Thomas Edison first introduced the phonograph to the public at Grand Hotel. Other notable happenings at Grand Hotel consist of the filming of two major movies, "This Time For

Keeps", staring Esther Williams and Jimmy Durante, and "Somewhere In Time", staring Christopher Reeves and Jane Seymour.

Since Grand Hotel was built, it is the first place many people notice when coming to the Island by boat. The hotel is a living time capsule of by-gone era, when long held traditions, such as requiring "proper" attire for dinner (coat & tie), were paramount. Further, it is an example of an architectural style and level of craftsmanship rarely found throughout the United States today. It is because of these qualities that the majestic hotel was declared a historic building by the state of Michigan in 1957 and, later in 1989, declared a National Landmark by the United States. Grand Hotel is a place that absolutely lives up to its name.

Ghostly Activity:

Many people have reported stories of unexplained phenomena at Grand Hotel over the years. In fact, the very grounds the hotel was constructed on contained numerous ancient Native American human skeletons, which have since been moved. This may explain some of the paranormal activity at the location. However, other activity is apparently not of Native American origin. Such is the following tale of a mysterious woman in black who once came to visit.

In 1891, a woman dressed in black clothing with a veil concealing her face, visited the hotel. She was accompanied only by a footman and maid-in-waiting. The woman in black never came out to socialize with other guests of the hotel. She only left the confines of her suite three times per day at 8am, 12 noon, and 7pm, to walk her large white Russian Wolfhound. She would walk her dog up and down the hotel's front porch for half an hour while guests, enjoying their meals in the main dining room, looked on. She was very secretive, never speaking a word, and no one seemed to know her true identity.

The woman in black left as swiftly as she had arrived. Some people reported a large black bird perched on the railing near the woman's room the day she departed. The woman never returned as a guest and her identity somehow remained a mystery.

Some guests of the hotel who dine near the windows in the main dining room have reportedly seen a woman dressed all in black walking a large white dog on the porch. Yet, as soon as the apparition is spotted, it vanishes before others can witness it.

The Porch of Grand Hotel.

Other paranormal activity found at Grand Hotel include orb sightings in several locations throughout the hotel. One of the most active areas seems to be in the lobby outside of the main dinning room. There have been several photos taken of the orbs at this location as well as in hallways near guestrooms.

One winter, when Grand Hotel was closed for the season, a maintenance worker on duty reported multiple phenomena such as footsteps in the hallways, faint voices or whispers, and doors opening and slamming shut on their own. The reason this was so unnerving was that the maintenance worker was alone in the massive hotel at the time of the occurrences.

Another ghost believed to haunt Grand Hotel is a young girl. The girl's name is reported to be Rebecca and she haunts the fourth floor of the hotel. Rebecca was a guest of the hotel with her family, when, reportedly, she accidentally fell to her death from her hotel room window. Apparently she is a friendly spirit and means no harm. Photos of orbs have been taken in the area she haunts.

The fourth floor hallway that Rebecca is believed to haunt.

Grand Hotel's Haunting & Ghostly Activity Scale:
Time Scale: ★ ★ ★
Intensity: ✳ ✳
Regularity: ✳ ✳

The Innkeeper of Metivier Inn

The Metivier Inn.

Location:

7466 Market Street
Downtown Mackinac Map Location # 3

Brief History:

The Metivier Inn is believed to have been originally built, or at least purchased, by Louis Joseph Metivier in 1877. Louis was a veteran of the Civil War and his family has a history with Mackinac Island dating back to the 1830's.

While living on Mackinac, Louis married Josephine Lambert in 1877. The two started a family and Louis found work as a lighthouse keeper. In 1902, while stationed away from his family at the Upper Range Light on the St. Mary's River, he suffered a fatal stroke. His wife Josephine was left to care for their children and the house.

With the insurance money Josephine received from her husband's death, she paid for his funeral, paid-off debts, and spent the remaining portion on repairs to the house. In order to provide for her family, Josephine converted the home to a boarding house and moved her family's living quarters into the back of the house.

Josephine's children grew up and moved on to have families of their own with one exception, Mary Sophia. Mary Sophia never married and agreed to care for her mother during her final years. In turn, the Metivier family decided that Mary would take ownership of the house when their mother passed away.

During her life, Josephine was well known for her warm hospitality and willingness to help those in need. Unfortunately, Josephine Metivier passed away March 7, 1935. She was fondly remembered by all the lives she touched.

Aside from becoming the owner of the house after the death of her mother, Mary Sophia Metivier also owned and operated a newsstand near the ferry docks. At the newsstand, she was one of the first people to greet tourists visiting Mackinac Island. She owned the Metivier home until her own death in 1959.

After Mary Sophia passed away, her youngest sister, Mabel, inherited the family home. After Mabel's death, her children inherited the home. Mabel's children ran the home as a dormitory for college-age employees of local hotels.

In 1985, the current owners purchased the Metivier house. They invested a large amount of money to convert the home from dormitory-style living quarters into the exceptional bed and breakfast it is today. In fact, The Metivier Inn has been recognized by numerous local and national travel publications as one of the best on the Island and in the State of Michigan.

Ghostly Activity:
    The ghost that dwells at the Metivier Inn is that of a kindly woman. She has been known to check on some of the guests staying at the inn. The most common occurrence seems to be her passing through a closed door into a room and remarking "just checking" to witnesses, before vanishing into thin air.
    Is this the ghost of one of the Metivier women? Perhaps it is Josephine, who was known for her kind ways. Or maybe it is Mary Sophia or Mabel. No one seems to be sure who the ghost is, but it is definitely a good spirit who wishes no harm to anyone.

Metivier Inn's Haunting & Ghostly Activity Scale:
Time Scale: ★ ★ ★
Intensity: ✶ ✶ ✶
Regularity: ✳ ✳

Village Inn

The Village Inn Restaurant and Lounge.

Location:
> *1384 Hoban Street.*
> *Downtown Mackinac Map Location # 5*

Brief History:
The Village Inn is one of the only year-round restaurants on Mackinac Island. It serves a wide selection of delicious dishes for breakfast, lunch, and dinner. Village Inn is famous for its Planked Whitefish entrée; yum!

The building that houses the Village Inn is relatively new compared to many others in the area. Constructed during the 1980's, the building itself has no notable historical significance. However, the land on which the building is located has a history. The property under the Village Inn was once occupied by St. Anne's church and cemetery (*see Island of The Dead, p.51*). During the 1800's the church and most, but not all b of the cemetery were moved to their current locations.

Ghostly Activity:

A former employee, who wishes to remain anonymous, recounts "strange things happening" when he worked at the restaurant. Most of the activity was limited to unusual goings-on with the electrical equipment. Could this activity have been from ghostly entities using the building's electrical system as an attempt to manifest (*see What Is A Ghost, p.9*)? Other reports claim that at times the place would "just not feel right", as if someone or something was there with you.

If it is true that several graves remain in the area of the Village Inn, could the ghosts of those forgotten so long ago remain? Perhaps the ghosts are looking for an answer as to why they were not moved with the rest of the cemetery. On the other hand, maybe they are just looking for something good to eat at the Village Inn.

Village Inn's Haunting & Ghostly Activity Scale:

Time Scale: ★ ★

Intensity: ✳

Regularity: ✳ ✳

Mister Shamus McNally

The McNally Bed and Breakfast.

Location:
> *7416 Main Street.*
> *Downtown Mackinac Map Location # 6*

Brief History:

McNally's Cottage was originally built in 1889 by Michael McNally as a home for his family. In the summer, Mr. McNally would rent out some of the rooms to tourists. Over the years, the home was converted to a bed and breakfast. This charming B&B is located right downtown and has wonderful, unobstructed, views of the Island's harbor and straits just beyond. The McNally family still owns and operates the bed and breakfast to this day.

Ghostly Activity:

The most well known ghostly encounter to take place at the McNally's was in 1990. A female guest at the bed and breakfast was looking out her window at the straits and worrying about a sickness she had. She was then touched on the shoulder and turned to see a short, older man standing in front of her. The old man told her not to worry and that "everything will be all right." The old man left her room and she thought nothing of it. The next day she came downstairs and found a picture of the man who she spoke with in her room. The man was Shamus McNally, one of Michael McNally's children. However, Shamus had passed away a number of years earlier and the woman had encountered his ghost. The comforting news Shamus shared with the woman came true; her sickness healed and "everything was all right."

McNally's Haunting & Ghostly Activity Scale:

Time Scale: ★ ★

Intensity: ✱ ✱ ✱

Regularity: ✱

The Lilac Tree

The Lilac Tree.

Location:

7372 Main Street

Downtown Mackinac Map Location # 7

Brief History:

One of the newest hotels on Mackinac Island, the Lilac Tree Hotel is a wonderful place to stay in the center of downtown. The Lilac Tree was built in the early 1990's and is an all suite hotel, and the property offers great views of both the Straits of Mackinac and the bustling downtown area.

As great as the Lilac Tree Hotel is, its location has a tragic past. On September 9, 1989, a fire broke out in the building that previously occupied the location, The LaSalle Building. The LaSalle Building was a turn-of-the-century property which housed seasonal workers and retail businesses. The fire destroyed several businesses and damaged others nearby. The real tragedy of the fire though, was the two lives that it claimed.

Most of the summer employees who lived in the LaSalle Building dormitory had already left for the season. However, one of the seven who had remained carelessly threw a lit cigarette into a trash can late one Friday night. The fire is believed to have begun slowly, developing into a huge blaze as it reached the dry wood of the nearly 100-year-old building. The blaze took approximately seven hours to bring under control. If the weather conditions that night had been dry and windy instead of rainy and calm, the fire could have destroyed most of the historic downtown area.

Firefighters who fought the blaze thought that the building had been evacuated with nobody left inside. Unfortunately, they were wrong. A man and woman who had an ongoing romantic relationship died together trying to escape from the building.

The investigation after the fire revealed why the two victims may have found themselves confused or trapped. The fire escape signs in the LaSalle Building dormitory lead to a stairway that had been boarded up for years. Would the couple have survived if they were able to use the blocked stairway? Their bodies were found just ten feet from the obstructed stairway and two feet from a window in a bathroom they failed to reach.

Following the fire, a probe was launched into the fire safety of not only the LaSalle Building, but also the rest of the buildings on Mackinac Island. Before the fire, there were no inspections required for buildings housing seasonal employees and hotels were inspected only for insurance purposes. The investigation found many code violations and the safety inspector threatened to keep businesses closed if they did not comply with the Island's updated fire codes. The winter of that year was spent bringing many of the buildings on Mackinac Island up to code because of the new laws.

The LaSalle Building was a loss and was eventually torn down. The new building in its place is home to the Lilac Tree Hotel and Spa, The Island Bookstore, Leather Corral, Betty's Gifts, Michigan Peddler, Great Turtle Toys, Roses 'n' Sadie, and Christmas Store.

Ghostly Activity:

Paranormal activity at the Lilac Tree Hotel has just recently begun to surface and there have not been many encounters. However, those who have witnessed ghostly activity there believe the two students who died in the tragic fire of the former LaSalle Building may have something to do with it. Some have also reported unexplainable experiences in the basement of the building which left them terrified.

Lilac Tree's Haunting & Ghostly Activity Scale:

Time Scale: ★ ★ ★
Intensity: ✳ ✳
Regularity: ✳ ✳

The Geary House

A sketch of the Geary House on Market Street.

Location:

> *7248 Market Street*
> *Downtown Mackinac Map Location # 8*

Brief History:

The Geary House, which is currently owned by Mackinac Island State Parks, was originally built in the early 1840's. The house has been home to numerous people over the years, but is named after a former resident named Matthew Geary. Mr. Geary was a man of many trades. Records show that he was a family man, Light Keeper, Justice of The Peace, and the local Fish Inspector. Matthew Geary lived in the house during the mid-1800's and passed away in the 1870's. In 1971, the Matthew Geary House was added to the National Registry of Historic Places. The Geary House was recently the home in which the Director of the Mackinac State Historical Park lived with his family.

Ghostly Activity:

There has reportedly been little activity at The Geary House for quite some time. However, one of the Island's most well known ghost stories took place there.

As the story states, Matthew Geary's funeral was held shortly after he died. It was attended by his friends and family as well as a young immigrant woman who was an employee of Mr. Geary's. The immigrant woman was on her way to the cemetery when she realized that she had left her gloves at the Geary house. She then decided to return to the house to get them. Arriving at the house, the woman opened the front door. Looking inside, she saw a familiar man descending the stairway toward her. However, something was not right; the man she saw could not possibly be there. The woman was now face to face with the ghost of Matthew Geary.

Since Mr. Geary's funeral, there has been an occasional story of unexplained sounds or such. However, none have been equal to the intensity found in Mr. Geary's former employee's tale of horror.

Geary House's Haunting & Ghostly Activity Scale:

Time Scale: ★

Intensity: ★★★

Regularity: ✳

Fort Mackinac

High above the harbor sits Fort Mackinac.

Location:
>*Above Marquette Park.*
>*Downtown Mackinac Map Location # 10*

Brief History:

In 1779, when the British Commander Patrick Sinclair saw the bluffs high above the water on Mackinac Island, he knew that it was a perfect location to construct a new fort. Almost immediately, work was started on the formidable Fort Mackinac. Its location high on the bluffs would prove to be effective in future battles fought there.

Throughout history, Fort Mackinac has been under the command of either the British or the United States. Although built by the British, the Fort was technically handed over to the United States just 3 years later under the Treaty of Paris. However, the commanding British officer, Captain Robinson *(see Robinson's Folly, p.146)*, did not vacate the Fort, and he stopped all further construction.

Under The Treaty of London (Jay's Treaty) in 1796, the British forces at Fort Mackinac were required to give the Fort to the U.S. and leave the premises. The Fort was left in a mess and needed to not only be finished, but also repaired. The U.S. maintained control of the Fort and Island until the War of 1812.

On July 17, 1812, early in the morning before dawn, the British forces, in combination with a number of Native American warriors, made landfall on Mackinac Island at the location now known as British Landing. The British, under General Isaac Brock's command, made their way through the interior of the Island to a hill above Fort Mackinac (currently where Fort Holmes is located). There he positioned both the soldiers and cannons for an attack on the Fort below.

As the U.S. soldiers awoke, it was clear that they were in a bad situation. With only 60 U.S. soldiers, they were caught unprepared, undermanned, and unaware of the battle about to take place. The Fort's commander, Lieutenant Porter Hanks, had no choice but to surrender to the British.

Only one attempt to regain the Fort was made by U.S. forces during the War of 1812. The attempt was made by both land and sea, under the command of Colonel George Croghan. The first attack was by a squadron of five U.S. ships, but the ship's cannons lacked the range to reach the lofty heights of the Fort, leaving the first ground attack unsuccessful. The first attack lasted two days before poor weather conditions caused the ships to pull back.

One week later, a second assault was made on the Fort. This attack was covertly made on the ground and lead by Major Andrew Holmes. The assault was not effective in recapturing Fort Mackinac. This attack resulted in 51 wounded and 13 dead U.S. soldiers, including Major Holmes.

After the failed attempts to capture Fort Mackinac, the U.S. troops tried to initiate a blockade of British supply ships to Mackinac Island. The gunboats USS Tigress and the USS Scorpion were positioned in the waters surrounding the Island but were ineffective and the British soon took control of the two ships. Consequently, British forces held onto Mackinac Island until the end of the war (1814).

About six months after the failed attempts to regain Mackinac Island, the Treaty of Ghent was signed which gave the Island and Fort back to the United States.

Once more under the control of the United States, Fort Mackinac would never again change hands or see another battle. However, the Fort did stay active up until its decommision in 1895. During those 80 years, the Fort was the location of a controversial murder (*The Ghostly Soldier of Rifle Range Trail, p.67*), a suicide, and a prison for Confederate sympathizers during the Civil War. Today, the Fort serves as one of Mackinac Island's most important historical sites. It is a living museum that is open to the public during the warmer months of the year.

Ghostly Activity:
    Fort Mackinac is, by far, one of the most haunted locations on the Island. A number of different ghosts still remain at the Fort and some can be rather active.

The Cowles Children
    Two ghosts which remain in the Officers' Hill Quarters are believed to be Josiah and Isabel Cowles. Both died at a young age while their father was stationed at Fort Mackinac. Josiah was only 5 months old when he passed away in 1884 from a gastrointestinal disease. Four years later Isabel joined him, five weeks after she celebrated her first birthday in 1888.

    The activity in the Hill Quarters has varied from the cries of ghostly babies to motion sensors detecting something when nobody is there. Other phenomena taking place here includes furniture moving on its own and ghostly lights appearing at night in the windows of the bedrooms once occupied by the children.

An interesting thing about this story is that the children's mother, Mary Cowles, is believed to be the ghost which haunts the two children's gravesites (*see The Woman Who Weeps, p.57*).

The Officers' Hill Quarters. The second floor windows where people have seen unexplainable activity.

The Officers' Stone Quarters

Built in 1780, this is the oldest original building in the State of Michigan. It is now used as the location for the Kid's Quarters and Tea Room.

At the end of every day in the Kid's Quarters, the toys, which are available for children to play with, are neatly put away. However, the next morning the toys are sometimes scattered around and appear as if someone has been "playing" with them during the night. Could the ghosts of the children who died here still play with their toys?

The North Sally Port Entrance of Fort Mackinac.

The Phantom Fifer/Piper

At the North Sally Port (entranceway) of Fort Mackinac, a strange sound is sometimes heard on foggy mornings. The sound you may hear is a fifer/piper softly playing a tune. If you look at the walls above North Sally Port, you may even see his ghostly figure walking back and forth. The fifer/piper has not been positively identified, but may be one of the following musicians who died while serving at the Fort: James Ervine (1811), Samuel Finnemore (1819), or Thomas Ward (1850).

The Black Hole and Guardhouse

Located in the floor of the Guardhouse near the entrance of the Fort is the Black Hole. Used as the Fort's only prison until 1828, the Black Hole claimed the life of at least one prisoner. Rumors that a skeleton was found in the ground of the Black Hole have also circulated.

There have been photos taken that show orbs in the Guardhouse, and there have been reports of substantial temperature drops even on hot days. These "cold spots" have no logical explanation and could be the ghost of the prisoner that died here over 200 years ago.

Murder!!!

The murder of Corporal Hugh Flinn from a gunshot delivered by Private James Brown took place in the mess hall of the Fort in 1828. The location of Private Brown's later execution remains a mystery *(see The Ghostly Soldier of Rifle Range Trail, p.67).*

The Hospital

A tourist recently took a photo inside the hospital and an unexplained ghostly leg appeared in the picture. Some people who have entered the hospital claim to feel sadness while there. Others insist the hospital still has an air of sickness and death from those who died there long ago.

Fort Mackinac's Haunting & Ghostly Activity Scale:

Time Scale: ★ ★ ★
Intensity: ✳ ✳ ✳
Regularity: ✳ ✳ ✳

The Ghostly Rider

A representation of the ghostly rider.

Location:
In carriages traveling to and from Fort Mackinac.

Ghostly Activity:
Some carriage drivers who make runs to and from Fort Mackinac after sunset have been witness to a ghostly passenger. The passenger has been described as wearing a soldier's uniform and remaining as silent as the grave. Many who have spotted this ghost, initially believe it to be one of many actors still in costume after working at the Fort. However, the soldier who rides inside the carriage as it makes its way toward the stables never remains long enough to reach the final destination. The passenger just vanishes with no trace as to who he is or where he came from.

Ghost Rider's Haunting & Ghostly Activity Scale:
Time Scale: ★★
Intensity: ✷✷✷
Regularity: ✷✷

Island House Hotel

The Island House Hotel.

Location:
> *6966 Main Street*
> *Downtown Mackinac Map Location # 12*

Brief History:

The oldest hotel on Mackinac Island in operation is the Island House. Built in 1852 by Charles O'Malley, the hotel was originally a beach resort located next to the water. However, the second owner, Captain Henry Van Allen, decided that the hotel would serve better to future expansion if it was moved to its current location about 300 feet from the waterfront.

The Van Allen family owned and operated the Island House until the late 1930's, when Rose Van Allen Webster, Henry's daughter, passed away. During the Van Allen period, not only was the hotel moved, but both the east and west wings, which have helped to define the image of the Island House, were constructed.

After Rose's death, the hotel remained unused for several years. In 1945, the Moral Re-Armament organization used the hotel for a short period before moving to its new conference center at Mission Point. The Island House again sat empty for a few years until the late 1940's when a group of investors purchased the property. A group known as Island House Incorporated proceeded to operate the hotel. However, over the years, the property was not properly cared for and some felt that it would have to be torn down. That was until three local businessmen decided to save the hotel.

In 1969, Harry and James Ryba, along with Victor Callewaert, decided to purchase and restore the Island House. They wanted to bring back the glorious hotel that the Island House once was. After all the renovations and restorations were completed in 1972, the hotel was reopened to the public. The next year the hotel was declared a Michigan Historical Landmark, ensuring its survival for generations to come.

Since the 1970's restoration, there have been numerous improvements to the Island House Hotel. Some of the additions include a new pool, sauna, and several more guest rooms. The Island House is a great place to stay if you enjoy the feel of a classic hotel with modern amenities.

Ghostly Activity:

There have been reports that there is the ghostly presence of a man at the Island House Hotel. It has been claimed that the man died at the hotel quite some time ago and decided to take up a permanent residence. The ghostly man is not known to be hostile and usually pays little or no attention to current guests. However, he has been known to move furniture throughout the building and, on rare occasions, appear to a lucky witness. Perhaps he feels compelled to return the hotel and its furniture to the way it was when he was a guest.

Island House Hotel's Haunting & Ghostly Activity Scale:

Time Scale: ★★

Intensity: ✳✳✳

Regularity: ✳

The St. Cloud

St. Cloud Dormitory.

Location:

6918 Main Street

Downtown Mackinac Map Location # 13

Brief History:

The St. Cloud was built during the 1800's in the Queen Anne style. It is one of the Island's oldest standing hotels, though it is no longer used for that purpose. Today the St. Cloud is used as a housing dormitory for employees of the Chippewa Hotel, Lilac Tree Hotel, and Pink Pony.

Ghostly Activity:

Many residents of what is now referred to as "The Cloud", have reported strange things happening during their stay. One of the most commonly known ghosts to haunt the building is a little girl. Nobody seems to know who she is, but over the years she has made her presence known to many. Some believe the ghostly little girl was murdered there long ago when the St. Cloud was a hotel. Others believe she is not alone in the building and that the person who murdered her is also still here.

Activity recently witnessed has varied from footsteps and balls bouncing down hallways to furniture floating in the middle of a room. One former resident claims that the ghosts in the building knocked over an entire bunk-bed when they entered their room. Those who live at The Cloud are no strangers to unusual activity and for the most part are comfortable with it. It has been reported that the ghosts are not trying to scare people and will stop if asked to do so.

St. Cloud's Haunting & Ghostly Activity Scale:

Time Scale: ★ ★ ★
Intensity: ✶ ✶ ✶
Regularity: ✳ ✳ ✳

Pine Cottage & Chateau Lorraine

Pine Cottage.

Location:

> *Pine Cottage*
> *1427 Bogan Lane*
> *Downtown Mackinac Map Location # 14*
>
> *Chateau Lorraine*
> *1432 Bogan Lane*
> *Downtown Mackinac Map Location # 15*

Brief History:

Pine Cottage has been welcoming guests since 1890. In its earlier days, several famous guests stayed there. Ty Cobb and Ernest Hemingway even spent their honeymoons at this charming hotel.

It is also claimed that Pine Cottage was the location of a murder which took place in 1942. Even though the story has several variations, many of the details remain the same, one being that a woman was murdered by a "large" man. Little else of the case is widely known. The case was never solved and the identity of the man remains a mystery.

Over the years, the hotel was converted to housing for members of Moral Re-armament (M.R.A.) group. Later, it was sold and the new owner used the property as a dormitory for both his family and employees. He then moved his employees across the street to what is now known as Chateau Lorraine and opened Pine Cottage as a place for tourists once again. Today, the hotel has been converted into a large bed and breakfast.

Ghostly Activity:

Pine Cottage is considered by some to be one of the most haunted locations on Mackinac Island. There have been numerous encounters here with as many as three or four different entities. No one is exactly sure when the ghostly activity began. However, the Moral Re-armament warned one owner when selling the property that the place was haunted. A majority of the activity here has been reported to occur in the fall.

The known ghosts that inhabit Pine Cottage are simply named, the "creature", the man, the woman, and the little girl.

The "Creature"

The "creature" has been described as looking like a man, but hunched over with horns lining his back. There have not been many sightings of this entity, and the most notable case of this creature is from one of the former owners of Pine Cottage.

The owner had a fight with his wife and went to another room to sleep. He awoke in the middle of the night when the blankets on the bed were pulled from him. Looking for the cause of the pulled blankets, he spotted the "creature" at the end of the bed staring at him. The man then hastily returned to his own bedroom where he spent a sleepless night with his wife, never to be bothered by the creature again.

The Woman

The ghostly woman appearing at Pine Cottage is believed to be the person murdered here in 1942. One of the most well known sightings was by a former owner of the property. The owner was going into room #4 when a woman rushed out of a closet, passed him, and went out the window. The strange thing about the woman was she had no visible legs and appeared to be flying. The owner's dog, who also witnessed the event, never entered room #4 again.

The ghostly woman may also be a historical repeater similar to the ghost of the man. However, the woman's ghost has done things that are not repeated. For example, she has been seen checking on guests staying at Pine Cottage. This activity appears to be more in line with a sentient spirit (*see Type of Ghosts, p.15*). Whatever the reason the ghostly woman has for being at Pine Cottage, she is not there to threaten anyone. She may be a restless spirit, but she is not an evil one.

The Man

The "large" man who haunts Pine Cottage remains unknown, but has been rumored to be the killer of the woman who also haunts the building. Ghostly activity from the man tends to be more frequent than the "creature" and includes opening and slamming doors, heavy footsteps, voices, and sometimes a full apparition.

The ghostly man seems to be angry and has been heard swearing in a coarse voice. Is he a historical repeater, playing out an argument from that dark rainy night in 1942, in which he committed murder? It seems to make sense, but unfortunately, the case has remained as mysterious as the ghostly activity which takes place here.

The Little Girl

The most active ghost at Pine Cottage is that of a little girl. The girl has been described as a sad young girl, with big eyes and long blonde hair. She has been encountered throughout Pine Cottage and is frequently seen across the street playing the piano at Chateau Lorraine. Why the little girl moves between Pine Cottage and Chateau Lorraine has remained a mystery. Some people on the street have even noticed her looking out the windows of Pine Cottage's attic.

The reason for the little girl's ghostly presence at Pine Cottage may be the result of neglectful parents. A neighbor of Pine Cottage once claimed that the little girl was the daughter of a couple who once lived there. Both parents were reportedly very heavy drinkers. As the story goes, the girl was left behind at Pine Cottage when her parents moved to Detroit. The girl is thought to have died soon after. Since then, her ghost has been seen weeping, and if asked what is wrong, she will reply, "Mommy, I want to come home."

The ghostly little girl's other home, Chateau Lorraine.

Pine Cottage & Chateau Lorraine's Haunting & Ghostly Activity Scale:
Time Scale: ★ ★ ★
Intensity: ✷ ✷ ✷
Regularity: ✻ ✻ ✻

Madame La Framboise

A sketch of Madeleine La Framboise.

Location:

> *Harbour View Inn*
> *6860 Main Street*
> *Downtown Mackinac Map Location # 16*

> *St. Anne's Church*
> *6836 Main Street*
> *Downtown Mackinac Map Location # 17*

Brief History:

Born in 1780 near the present day city of Grand Haven, Michigan, Madeleine La Framboise was the daughter of a French-Canadian fur trader and an Ottawa Native American woman. She was married in 1794 to a prominent businessman, Joseph La Framboise, in a traditional Ottawa wedding ceremony. The next year, in September, their daughter Josette was born.

Madeleine, Joseph, Josette, and later, son Joseph Jr., settled on Mackinac Island. While on the Island, Madeleine and Joseph were married again in 1804, only this time it was "official" and took place at St. Anne's Church. Madeleine would spend most of her life on the Island. She was a devoted member of St. Anne's Church and may have been responsible for saving the church from financial ruin at one time. Her close connection with the Church would play a significant role throughout her life, even affecting her after her death.

In 1806, Madeleine's husband, Joseph, was away on business when he was murdered by an intoxicated Native American named White Ox after Joseph refused to give him more liquor. White Ox was captured and brought to Madeleine who showed him mercy by granting his release, his only punishment being permanent banishment from his Native American tribe. Joseph was buried near present day Grand Haven, but later Madeleine had his body exhumed and brought him back to Mackinac Island.

The death of Madeleine's husband changed her life. Instead of selling the extensive businesses her husband owned, she decided to run them herself; an uncommon choice for a woman of that time. She found great success in fur trading and made her mark on the industry. In 1820, she decided to retire from the business and spent most of her time on Mackinac Island where she was better known as Madame La Framboise.

While Madame La Framboise was enjoying her time on Mackinac Island, her daughter, Josette, married the commander of Fort Mackinac, Captain Benjamin Pierce. Captain Pierce, a relative of former President of the United States, Franklin Pierce, was a generous man. He helped construct a home for his mother-in-law and blessed her with a granddaughter, Harriet (1817). The home, which still

stands today, is now a cozy historic hotel called The
Harbour View Inn.

Harbour View Inn.

Not long after the home was constructed,
Madeleine's daughter, Josette, died while giving birth to her
second child (1820), a boy named Langdon. The infant died
soon after and both were buried on the land where St.
Anne's Church now stands. Captain Pierce left the Island for
reassignment in Florida, leaving his daughter, Harriet, in the
care of her grandmother.

Over the years, Madeleine remained an active
member of St. Anne's Church. She donated not only her
time as a catechism teacher, but some land for a new
location for the Church. This land is where St. Anne's
Church is currently located, across the street from
Madeleine's former home.

On April 4, 1846, Madeleine's health failed and she passed away. She was buried next to her daughter and grandson under St. Anne's Church.

The next occurrence, that took place, is believed to be the cause of Madeleine La Framboise's restless spirit. During the mid 1950's, St. Anne's decided to construct a basement underneath the current building. The problem was that Madeleine, Josette, and Langdon's remains were all buried under the Church altar. Therefore, in order for the basement to be built, the remains had to be moved.

It is believed that the earthly remains of Madeleine, Josette, and Langdon were stored in a barn for several years. Finally, after the pleading of relatives, the three were laid to rest in the Churchyard.

Ghostly Activity:

Several different phenomena have taken place since the remains of Madeleine, Josette, and Langdon have been disturbed.

The first took place soon after the basement was built under the Church. The foundation of the Church weakened so severely following construction that the walls began to slump and the plaster cracked. Although repaired, some have attributed this dilemma to a curse Madeleine may have placed on the Church for upsetting her final resting place.

The second paranormal phenomenon involves Madeleine's house and tombstone. Since the remains were moved to the Churchyard, her house and tombstone have been reported to possess a ghostly "glow" in some photographs. The glow has been described as if the stone was on fire surrounded by red, yellow, and orange lights.

The last known incident of paranormal phenomena occurred in Madeleine's house before it was converted into the Harbour View Inn. A video tape of the entire interior of the house was made. When the tape was played back, the footage was present except for a gap several minutes in length. The gap showed nothing, just a blank screen. The missing footage was that of Madeleine La Framboise's bedroom. Nothing else was missing from the video.

La Framboise's Haunting & Ghostly Activity Scale:

Harbour View Inn
Time Scale: ★★
Intensity: ✹✹
Regularity: ✹

St. Anne's Church
Time Scale: ★★
Intensity: ✹✹
Regularity: ✹

Bailey Cottage

Bailey Cottage as it is today.

Location:

> *1378 Church Street*
> *Downtown Mackinac Map Location # 18*

Brief History:

Built during the 1800's, this property has been used as a boarding house for tourists, local workers, and other types of travelers throughout most of its history. However, the building is believed to have once housed both a brothel and later, during prohibition, an illegal distillery. In fact, the ceiling in the attic is supposedly still charred from the burning stills below.

Once, while named Terrace Cottage, the building was used as a brothel. In fact, a photo exists of Terrace Cottage which is said to include several of the house's prostitutes. Allegedly, one of the prostitutes committed suicide by hanging herself in the turret room of the house.

Reportedly, a former owner also suffered a tragic death in the building. The story states that the man, named Bill, was smoking a pipe in the living room when he unfortunately drifted off to sleep. The pipe fell and started a fire which engulfed him.

Recently the building has been used to house Island employees. These same employees are the people who reported the ghostly activity at the Bailey Cottage.

Ghostly Activity:

The activity at the Bailey Cottage has varied from doors opening and closing on their own, to footsteps and objects falling off countertops. Occasionally, the residents of Bailey Cottage have heard human voices coming from an otherwise vacant second floor. There is also activity in the attic above the bedrooms. At times, sounds of boxes or equipment moving around can be heard at times. It may be the ghosts of those who operated the illegal distillery, continuing their work long after passing on.

The most unnerving ghost in the building is the woman who peeks into bedrooms. The ghost has not been identified, but the residents believe she is the prostitute who died there many years ago. Occasionally, as a resident is in their bedroom, her ghost will appear in the doorway only to vanish upon being discovered. This ghost also has been known to shake people's beds and pull at their sheets as they try to sleep.

Bailey Cottage Haunting & Ghostly Activity Scale:
Time Scale: ★ ★ ★
Intensity: ✸ ✸ ✸
Regularity: ✴ ✴ ✴

The Mission House Ghosts

The Mission House.

Location:
1246 Franks Street
Downtown Mackinac Map Location # 21

Brief History:

The Mission House, originally built in 1825 by Reverend William M. Ferry and his wife, Amanda, served as a boarding school for over 500 children during its time. A majority of those children were Native American or a Native American and Euro-American mix called Métis.

The Mission House School was run like one big family. When a child became sick, medical attention was provided by the doctor stationed at Fort Mackinac. However, some medical methods of that time were questionable and very likely led to the deaths of several children. During the school's operating years, there were a total of sixteen known deaths among students, most from illnesses. The recorded names of the children who died in the Mission House are:

1824	*Sarah Barrett(8)*
1826	*Joseph Lyman(12)*
1827	*Electa Hastings(15), Samuel Lasley(4), Isaac Miller(10)*
1828-1829	*John Christie(4), Charlotte Deverney(16), Hervey Lavette(8), Louis Pyant(7), Peter Pyant(5), Margaret Sayre(8), John Sayre(12), Robert Sayre(6), Eliza Warner(8)*
1830	*Mary Lyon Grant(?)*
Year ?	*Heydenburk (baby)* *(Rock from a cliff fell on him.)*

(These names may not reflect the children's actual names since it was common practice for an English name to be assigned to students of French or Native American heritage.)

In 1845, Edward A. Franks purchased the old Mission House School, added an additional floor, and converted it into a hotel. The hotel was opened for business in 1849 and housed tourists and guests on the Island until it closed in 1939.

For the next seven years, the building was used to house local employees. Then in 1946, Miles Philimore and his wife, Margaret, attained ownership and used the Mission House as a home for the Moral Re-Armament Movement. As stated earlier in the book, the purpose of this group was defined as "the good road of an ideology inspired by God upon which all can unite. Catholic, Jew or Protestant, Hindu, Muslim, Buddhist and Confucians - all find they can change, where needed, and travel along this good road together." Some believe this group was an early version of Alcoholics Anonymous.

An attempt was made in the early 1970's by evangelist Rex Humbard and his Cathedral of Tomorrow to turn the property into a religious retreat for members of his congregation. The retreat was not a success and was soon sold to the State. Today the State of Michigan still owns the Mission House and uses the property to house employees of the Mackinac Island State Park.

Ghostly Activity:

It is believed that some of the Native American or Métis children, who became ill and died when the Mission House was a boarding school, still haunt its rooms and hallways today.

Those who have witnessed the Mission House ghosts have reported forms that resemble young children throughout the first two floors and basement. The third floor has had very little activity, most likely because it was added in 1845 after the school closed down (*ghostly entities usually only haunt what was familiar to them in life*).

No one is exactly sure whom of the original Mission House children haunt this building, but one common sighting is of a small boy. He enjoys watching people until they spot him and then runs away. One state employee witnessed this ghost one night in the hallway while getting some water. He described the experience as the scariest sight in his life.

Other ghostly children have also been seen wandering the halls at night and occasionally during the day. The playful spirits have knocked over alarm clocks and sporadically woken people up by bumping into their beds in the middle of the night. Although the ghosts here are not hostile or aggressive, they want people to know they are present.

Sightings at the Mission House are recent and employees of the Mackinac Island State Park who have lived there over the past few summers have repeatedly reported that they have "seen things" that just could not be explained.

Mission House's Haunting & Ghostly Activity Scale:
Time Scale: ★ ★ ★
Intensity: ✹ ✹ ✹
Regularity: ✹ ✹ ✹

The Last Gathering of Giant Fairies

Mission Point.

Location:

 Off Main Street (Huron) at the East end of
Downtown, in front of Mission Point Resort.
Downtown Mackinac Map Location # 22

Brief History:

 The area in front of Mission Point has served several
purposes over the years. Native Americans used the location
as both a summer home and burial ground. During the last
century it has, at one time or another, been a part of the
Moral Re-Armament Movement, Mackinac College, and
Mission Point Resort. However, according to local legend,
it was originally used as a gathering place for the Giant
Fairies.

Legendary Tale:

Native Americans have long regarded Mackinac Island as the former home to an ancient race of giants. Today, all that remains of that race is the giant rock formations into which they were transformed.

The last time the giants were reportedly seen by human eyes was sometime in the 1800's. The last person to witness the giants' final gathering was a teacher at the Mission House School. The teacher remains anonymous, but the story he told is remarkable.

As the teacher's story goes, he was sitting on the porch at Mission House, enjoying the end of a beautiful day, when suddenly he saw giants descend from the cliffs behind the school. They were gathering on the grass near the lake dressed in elaborate gowns and capes made of butterfly wings, feathers of rare plumage, and other exotic materials. He stated that what he witnessed was "amazing and otherworldly."

The event the teacher was about to witness was a wedding of mythical proportions. The field became vibrant when enormous fireflies colorfully lit up the festivities and the flowers turned silver and rang as bells. Under a gigantic flower serving as a tent, the ceremony began. Truly, this was a sight to behold.

As the night progressed, the giants ran out of wine. The teacher, not wanting the party to end, threw a bottle of his own wine to the giants. As the bottle reached them, it grew to the size of a "hogshead." The bottle frightened the giants and one of them approached the teacher. "Thou art a mortal! A human brother! We are the remnants of the first children of the earth. Our race is nearly extinct. As living creatures tonight, we pass away, yet do not entirely leave the earth, but take shape and dwell in the rocks and boulders, cliffs and mountains. We have never yet allowed a mortal to keep his eyes after looking upon our gatherings; but as this is to be our last meeting, and as thou hast a good heart, and hast wished to prolong our cheer, thou art welcome to come among us without fear of harm," said the giant. The teacher accepted the invitation.

The teacher danced with the giants and even the bride. He drank and partook of all their festivities. Suddenly, it began to rain and the giants ran away. The teacher screamed, "A deluge!" and woke to find himself lying in the grass near the water. There was no sign of the giants, no fireflies, no flower tent; nothing. Instead, the teacher, who was surrounded by an abundant supply of empty wine bottles, peered up at the Mission House housekeeper who was now holding an empty water pail.

For days, the schoolteacher sat on the porch with a large supply of wine, with hopes that the giants would return. They never did. The giants had left to become the large rocks and spires of cliffs we see today.

Mission Point Resort

Mission Point Resort.

Location:
> *6396 Main Street*
> *Downtown Mackinac Map Location # 23*

Brief History:

It was in 1825 that Reverend William M. Ferry founded the Mission school, and later church, which Mission Point is named after. Mission Point encompasses the entire southeast tip of Mackinac Island and has been the location of several different endeavors prior to becoming Mission Point Resort.

The land the resort stands on today is the location Dr. Frank Buchman chose to build The Moral Re-Armament (MRA) World Conference Center. The M.R.A. movement was founded on the philosophy of "the Four Absolutes" which consisted of honesty, purity, unselfishness, and love. The group built most of what is now Mission Point Resort through the 1950's.

In 1966, the MRA moved its operations to Switzerland, leaving the land and buildings to Mackinac

College. The college, which lasted only four years, was a fully accredited four-year school. Unfortunately, Mackinac College came into financial trouble and only graduated one class in 1970.

The following owner of the Mission Point Resort area was Rex Humbard. Humbard, a televangelist, purchased Mission Point in 1970 for use as a spiritual retreat for himself and members of his congregation. The retreat was short lived and closed two years later.

In 1972, Mission Point became a hotel and resort for tourists. Since the 1970's the resort has undergone several name changes, a few owners, and various renovations. The resort's soundstage and lodging were used in 1979 for the production of the movie "Somewhere In Time."

Today, the resort is called Mission Point Resort and has all the amenities one would come to expect. The current owner purchased the property in 1987. Since the purchase, there have been a number of impressive improvements to the resort. This is a great place to stay if you want to get away from the downtown tourist activity and just relax.

Ghostly Activity:

Mission Point has long been the location of legend and lore. Therefore, it seems fitting that the location is home to several ghostly spirits.

In the years since Mission Point was home to Mackinac College, a tragic story of a young man has been passed down. The story tells of Harvey, a student at Mackinac College, and his love for a fellow female classmate. The two students dated, but unfortunately, the girl was not romantically interested in Harvey and broke off their relationship. Harvey's heart was broken. Deciding that life was no longer worth living, he climbed to the top of the bluffs behind Mission Point and threw himself off.

Harvey's ghost remains at Mission Point and has been seen in numerous locations around the resort. His ghost is well known for mischievous behavior among the resort staff. Some staff have reported that after cleaning up an area of the resort, they have returned to find it a mess again. Overall, Harvey's ghost has become more of an annoyance and has never harmed anyone.

Mission Point Theater. A popular place to spot "Harvey."

Other ghosts have reportedly been sighted at Mission Point Resort around the theater. Some have seen ghostly soldiers from Fort Mackinac walking, or even patrolling, the area. When approached, they vanish.

Mission Point Resort's Haunting & Ghostly Activity Scale:
Time Scale: ★ ★ ★
Intensity: ✳ ✳ ✳
Regularity: ✳ ✳ ✳

Ghostly Guests At Small Point Cottage

A view of Small Point Cottage.

Location:

6220 Main Street
Downtown Mackinac Map Location # 24

Brief History:

The last building on eastbound Huron (Main) Street, before you reach the State Park, is Small Point Cottage. The only example of gothic revival architecture left on the Island, Small Point Cottage is a wonderfully charming bed and breakfast. It is far enough away from the large crowds and noise of the downtown area to allow oneself to just relax and enjoy the serenity.

The house was originally built in 1882 by Alanson and Ann Sheely, who also built an identical house nearby. The house was moved in the 1950's in order for the Moral

Re-Armament World Conference Center to be built. Currently, the Mission Point Theater is located where the Sheely house once was. The sister house was torn down.

Over the years, there have been a number of different owners of the home. One of the owners had a young daughter who was deeply saddened when her family had to move away. However, in 1971, John Findlay, the current owner, moved to Mackinac Island with his family. He was hired as an elementary school teacher on the Island and needed a home that could fit his large family as well as handle the Island's harsh winters; Small Point Cottage was the answer. Over the years, as the Findlay children grew up and moved out, the home was converted to a bed and breakfast.

Today, the B&B is still owned by the Findleys and open to guests during the warmer months.

Ghostly Activity:

Some of those who have either worked at Small Point Cottage or stayed as a guest have become familiar with the two resident ghosts found there. Both ghosts are neither victims of a tragedy or horrible death, but were forced, for one reason or another, to leave Small Point Cottage. Both loved Small Point Cottage and Mackinac Island so much that after passing away, they returned to the place they once called home.

The first ghost is believed to be the daughter of a previous owner of Small Point Cottage who, after her family had to move away, declared that she would one day return. It is commonly believed that this ghost is that same little girl who fulfilled her promise to return to the place she loved.

The ghostly little girl has been here long before Small Point Cottage became a Bed and Breakfast. She is a non-threatening presence, and is known to move items, sometimes even taking them for her "collection." Her footsteps can be heard throughout the house and, occasionally, she makes other unexplainable noises. Guests who have experienced the girl's ghost claim that she is playful and pleasant.

The second ghost residing at Small Point Cottage is a man known only as "Aaron." He, too, is believed to have once lived at the house, developing a strong attachment toward it. Aaron is considered to be a gentle spirit and has always been non-threatening.

Aaron is notorious for creating his own personal mischief around Small Point Cottage. His most common activities include footsteps, doors opening and closing, and the locking of the front door (which stopped when the owner asked him to). Occasionally, he will appear to someone as an apparition, but this is far less common.

Small Point Cottage's Haunting & Ghostly Activity Scale:

Time Scale: ★ ★ ★
Intensity: ✴ ✴ ✴
Regularity: ✴ ✴

Robinson's Folly

Looking up at Robinson's Folly.

Location:
> *High up on a bluff overlooking Small Point Cottage*
> *and Mission Point Resort.*
> *Downtown Mackinac Map Location # 25*

Brief History:
Robinson's Folly is named after the British commander of Fort Mackinac, Captain Daniel Robinson, who served there from 1782 - 1787. Standing a towering

127 feet above the lake, Robinson's Folly is the setting of several tragic tales and a ghost story.

Tragic Tales:

1.   While Captain Robinson served at Fort Mackinac, he fell in love with a beautiful Native American woman named Wintemoyen. Wintemoyen was, unfortunately, promised, by her father Peezhiki, to another Native American man, Assibun. But Wintemoyen could not stand the thought of having to marry Assibun.

Upon being informed of his lover's situation Robinson took her to his post on Mackinac Island. Soon afterwards Robinson and Wintemoyen were secretly married. They lived happily for a short time in a secluded cottage on the Island's eastern bluff. Robinson chose this location believing it would be a secure position and easy to guard if anyone from his wife's tribe decided to track them down.

Soon after Robinson and his bride were married, Assibun learned of the wedding. Furious, he tracked her to the cottage where she lived with her new husband.

Quietly, Assibun made his way to the cottage without detection. With no guard to be found, he peered through the window to find Wintemoyen happily waiting for her husband to come home. While the sun was setting, he entered the cottage. Wintemoyen knew her fate as soon as she saw Assibun. He ran his knife deep into the heart of the weeping bride, killing her.

As the murderer turned to leave, Robinson entered the cottage door. He immediately attacked Assibun and the two struggled with each other for some time. Eventually, they came dangerously close to the edge of the bluff when, suddenly, the two lost their balance and fell to their deaths.

Some say you can still find rocks under Robinson's Folly stained with the blood of the two men who died there.

2.   The above tale has also been told with a different outcome. In the second version, Robinson and Wintemoyen are married at Robinson's Folly.

After they had made their vows and the celebration began, Wintemoyen's father, Peezhiki, arrived. He had learned that his daughter had disobeyed his wishes and married the white man Robinson instead of Assibun. Peezhiki attacked Robinson and a fight ensued.

Robinson eventually overpowered Peezhiki and threw him off the cliff, but Peezhiki managed to grab a tree limb on the side of the cliff and held on for his life. Running to her father's aid, Wintemoyen tragically fell to her death; her father fell soon after.

3.   The last tale tells of a cottage once owned by Robinson that fell off the bluff. It is believed that the cottage was built close to the edge of the cliff before either a storm or minor earthquake caused the ground beneath it to give way. The cottage came tumbling down to the lakeshore along with the rock that it once sat upon. This attempts to explain why Robinson's Folly is seen today with an exposed patch of rock on its cliff.

Ghostly Activity:

Although there have been no current sightings of any ghosts, there is a legend about one.

When Fort Mackinac was an active military post, a soldier (possibly Captain Robinson) was out for a walk high up on the east bluff. The soldier suddenly spotted a beautiful Native American woman in the woods. He tried to speak to her, but she said nothing in return. As he tried to approach the woman, she fled. Giving chase, the soldier eventually cornered her at the location of Robinson's Folly.

Although, he meant her no harm and only wanted to know who this woman was, the beautiful woman was now perilously close to the edge of the cliff. The soldier was worried she might fall, so he lunged to grab her. But as he surged forward, the beautiful woman vanished with a cruel laughter and the poor soldier fell over the edge of the cliff to his death.

Again, no recent sightings of this apparition have been reported. However, if you see a beautiful woman in the woods near Robinson's Folly, use caution and do not chase her over the edge of the cliff.

Robinson's Folly Haunting & Ghostly Activity Scale:

Time Scale: ★

Intensity: ★★★

Regularity: ✳

Epilogue

I hope you enjoyed reading about the ghost stories, legends, and tragic tales which surround the Mackinac Island region. I know I enjoyed the research and writing involved with them.

In writing this book I found that there is more to ghost stories and legends than just hype and horror. As demonstrated in this book, history has a close bond with ghostly activity. The older a civilized area is the more likely ghosts have established a presence. Thus it is only natural that Mackinac, with thousands of years of Native American history and nearly three hundred years of modern history, is a prime location for ghosts. Mackinac's history continues to be written with each passing day and more ghosts are certain to follow.

SOURCES

Books

Andrews, Roger.
Old Fort Mackinac: on the hill of history. Herald- Leader Press.
Menominee, Mich. 1938.

Armour, David A.
100 Years At Mackinac: A centennial history of the Mackinac Island State Park Commission 1895-1995. 1995.

Arnold, Gustavus.
Grand Hotel, its romance and its mystery: A thumbnail sketch of fact and legend that has made this hostelry one of the outstanding institutions of America. Fireside Printing & Publishing Co., Detroit, Mich., 1957.

Barfknecht, Gary W.
Unexplained Michigan Mysteries: strange but true tales from the Michigan unknown. Friede Publications, Davision, Mich. 1993.

Burton, C.M.
LaSalle and the Griffon. Detroit. 1903.

Catherwood, Mary H.
Mackinac & Lake Stories. Harper & Brothers, New York, London, 1899.

Feltner, Charles E. & Jeri Baron.
Shipwrecks of the Straits of Mackinac. Seajay Publishing, Dearborn, Mich., 1991.

Franklin, Dixie.
Haunts of The Upper Great Lakes. Thunder Bay Press, Holt, Mich.. 1997.

Gringhus, Dirk.
Lore of The Great Turtle: Indian Legends of Mackinac Retold. Mackinac Island State Park Commission, Mackinac Island, Mich., 1970.

Kane, Grace F.
Myths and Legends of The Mackinaws. (1887). Black Letter Press, Grand Rapids, Mich., 1972.

Kelton, Lieut. D.H.
Annals of Fort Mackinac. Fergus Printing Company, Chicago, Ill., 1882.

Page, Lorena M.
Legendary lore of Mackinac: original poems of Indian legends of Mackinac Island. Lorena M. Page, Cleveland, Oh., 1901.

MacLean, Harrison John.
The Fate of The Griffon. Swallow Press. Chicago, Ill.. 1974.

McDowell, John E.
Madame La Framboise, Michigan History, vol. 56 (Winter 1972). Michigan Department of State. Lansing, Mich., 1972.

McVeigh, Amy.
Mackinac Connection: an insider's guide. Mackinac Publishing, Mackinac Island, Mich., 1998.

Macharg, William & Balmer, Edwin.
The Indian Drum. Grosset & Dunlap. New York, NY. 1917.

Mackinac Island Chamber of Commerce.
Discover Mackinac Island. 2001.

Petersen, Eugene T.
Historic Mackinac Island Visitors Guide. Mackinac Island State Park Commission, Mackinac Island, Mich., 1994.
Petersen, Eugene T.
Mackinac Island: Its history in pictures. Mackinac Island State Park Commission. Mackinac Island, Mich. 1973.

Porter, Phil.
Mackinac: An Island Famous in These Regions. Mackinac Island State Parks, Mackinac Island, Mich., 1998.

Porter, Phil.
Mackinac History: A Continuing Series of Illustrated Vignettes: Mackinac Island's Post Cemetery. Mackinac Island State Parks, Mackinac Island , Mich., 1999.
Porter, Phil.
View From The Veranda: The History and Architecture of the Summer Cottages on Mackinac Island. 1981.

Ratigan, William.
Straits of Mackinac! Crossroads of the Great Lakes. Wm. B. Eerdmans Publishing Company. Grand Rapids MI. 1957.

The Standard Guide: Mackinac Island and Northern Lake Resorts. Foster & Reynolds, 1899.

Vanfleet, J.A.
Summer Resorts of The Mackinac Region and Adjacent Localities. Lever Print, Detroit, Mich., 1882.

Widder, Keith R.
Battle for the soul : Métis children encounter evangelical Protestants at Mackinaw Mission, 1823-1837. Michigan State University Press, East Lansing, Mich., 1999.

Widder, Keith R.
Justice at Mackinac: the execution of Private James Brown. Mackinac Island State Park Commission, Mackinac Island, Mich., 1974.

Widder, Keith R.
Reveille Til' Taps: soldier life at Fort Mackinac, 1780-1895. Mackinac Island State Park Commission, Mackinac Island, Mich., 1972.

Williams, Meade C.
Early Mackinac: A Sketch Historical and Descriptive. Duffield & Company, New York, NY., 1912.

Wood, Edwin O.
Historic Mackinac. The MacMillian Company, New York, NY., 1918.

Newspapers

18 Men Lost. (1892, November 2). *Detroit Evening News.*

Abraham, Molly.
(1998, April 23). Southfield Man Leaps To Death Off Span. *Detroit Free Press.*

Around The Lakes. (1878, June 27). *Detroit Free Press.*

Around The Lakes. (1878, June 28). *Detroit Free Press.*

Associated Press.
(1990, March 22). 2 Charged In Fatal Mackinac Island Fire Attorney General Cites House's Owners. *Detroit Free Press.*

Associated Press.
(1989, October 28). Mackinac Probe: 557 Fire Code Violations. *Detroit Free Press.*

Associated Press.
(2000, September 11). Woman Jumps Off Bridge To Her Death. *Associated Press.*

Campbell, Bob.
(1987, Sept. 8). Bay City Man Dies After Mackinac Bridge Leap. *Detroit Free Press.*

Gould, Karen.
(2005, August 6). Island Cemeteries Provide Backdrop for Tombstone Tales. *Mackinac Island Town Crier.*

Gould, Karen.
(2006, April 15). State Park Rents Dock, Geary House. *Mackinac Island Town Crier.*

Hacker, David.
(1989, September 12). Couple Inches From Unlocked Window "Would Have Been No Problem In Getting Out" For Island Fire Victims. *Detroit Free Press.*

Hacker, David.
(1989, September 11). Couple Killed In Fire Was 'Perfect For Each Other'. *Detroit Free Press.*

Hacker, David & Zablit, Elyne.
(1989, September 10). Fire Hits Mackinac Island 2 Summer Workers
Killed. *Detroit Free Press.*
Hacker, David.
(1989, September 20).Fire Marshals To Check Safety Of Mackinac
Summer Housing. *Detroit Free Press.*

In Collision. (1892, November 3). *Detroit Evening News.*

Kirk, Robert D.
(1965, May 8). Comb Shore, Isle For Ship Survivors. *Detroit News.*

Lost!. (1892, November 2). *Cleveland Press*

Lost In The Gales!. (1887, October 4). *Detroit Evening News.*

Martin, Jeff & Matthew, Davis G.
(1997, March 3). At Least One Dies As Vehicle Falls Off Mackinac
Bridge. *Detroit Free Press.*

Miller, Holly G.
(1995, September-October). Get To The Point. *Saturday Evening Post.*

Mittendorf, Jeff.
(1997, October 31). Big Mac Turns 40. *Capital News Service.*

Mrs. Connerton's Story of The Wreck of The California. (1887,
October 7). *Detroit Evening News.*

Mystery Plane Rams 'Big Mac'. (1978, September 11). *Detroit News.*

Police Divers Find 3 Bodies After 'Big Mac' Plane Crash. (1978,
September 12). *Detroit News.*

Simmons, Boyd.
(1960, July 29). Find Widow Strangled In Mackinac Mystery. *Detroit
News.*

Snell, Robert.
(2002, August 23). Police End Search For Mother, Infant. *Lansing State
Journal.*

St. John, Paige.
(1990, April 2). Mackinac Island Battles Image As Firetrap. *Detroit Free Press.*

Staff and Wire Reports.
(2002, August 16). Mackinac Bridge Jumper Sought. *Traverse City Record -Eagle.*

Story of The Wreck. (1887, October 5). *Detroit Evening News.*

The California's Victims- Conflicting Statements. (1887, October 6). *Detroit Evening News.*

The Lost California. (1887, October 5). *Detroit Evening News.*

Volgenau, Gerry.
(2000, June 11). A Haan's Full Of History. *Detroit Free Press.*

Volgenau, Gerry.
(2000, June 11). Bogan Lane Hosts A Ghost. *Detroit Free Press.*

Volgenau, Gerry.
(2000, June 11). McNally's Has 7 Rooms, 1 Presence. *Detroit Free Press.*

Widow Vanishes; Dogs Join Hunt On Mackinac. (1960, July 26). *Detroit News.*

Zacharias, Pat.
The Breathtaking Mackinac Bridge. *The Detroit News.*

Zyble, Lisa.
(2004, December 11). Looking Back. *Mackinac Island Town Crier.*

Internet

Bilbey Publications.
"Waugoshance Light" *NorthernMichigan.com.* 9 August 2003. 9 August 2003.
http://www.northernmichigan.com/public/lighthouses/lakemichigan/waugoshance/waugoshancelight.html.

Beautiful Disaster
"Has Anyone Else Seen A Ghost." *I Survived Mackinac Island.* 17 April, 2006. 21 April, 2006. http://forum.myspace.com.

"Facts and Figures." *Mackinac Bridge Authority.* 1 January 2002. 9 August 2003. http://www.mackinacbridge.org/.

"FAQ History." *Mackinac Bridge Authority.* 1 January 2002. 9 August 2003. http://www.mackinacbridge.org/.

"Fort Mackinac." *Wikipedia.* Oct. 21, 2005. Nov. 12, 2005. http://en.wikipedia.org/wiki/Fort_Mackinac.

Ghost and Hauntings Research Society.
"Our "How To" Guide for Ghost Investigations." *The Toronto Ghosts and Hauntings Research Society.* March 19, 2006. April 2, 2006. http://www.torontoghosts.org/courses.htm.

Graham, Robert.
"California." *Historical Collections of the Great Lakes Vessels Online Index University Libraries / Bowling Green State University.* 1 February 2000. 17 September 2002. http://digin.bgsu.edu/cgi-win/vsl95x.exe.

Graham, Robert.
"Cedarville." *Historical Collections of the Great Lakes Vessels Online Index University Libraries / Bowling Green State University.* 1 February 2000. 17 September. http://digin.bgsu.edu/cgi-win/vsl95x.exe.

Graham, Robert.
"W.H. Gilcher." *Historical Collections of the Great Lakes Vessels Online Index University Libraries / Bowling Green State University.* 1 February 2000. 17 September. http://digin.bgsu.edu/cgi-win/vsl95x.exe.

Graham, Robert.
"Eber Ward." *Historical Collections of the Great Lakes Vessels Online Index University Libraries / Bowling Green State University.* 1 February 2000. 17 September 2002. http://digin.bgsu.edu/cgi-win/vsl95x.exe.

"Grand Hotel (Mackinac Island)." *Wikipedia.* March 28, 2006. April 3, 2006. http://en.wikipedia.org/wiki/Grand_Hotel_(Mackinac_Island).

Hamp, Patricia.
"Mackinac Marriage Record". *MIGenWeb.* May 15, 2006. May 20, 2006. http://www.rootsweb.com/~migenweb/.

"Harbour View Inn." *Harbour View Inn.* 17 April 2006. 1 October 2002. http://www.harbourviewinn.com/.

"Haunted Places In Michigan." *Shadowlands.* January, 2006. February 17, 2006. http://www.theshadowlands.net/places/michigan.htm.

"Historical Dates In Michigan's History April." *The Michigan Historical Society.* August 2003. 8 August 2003.
http://www.hsmichigan.org/pdf/tl_apr02.pdf#search='the%20historical%20society%20of%20michigan%20april%201974%20suicide'.

"History of The MRA And Mission Point Resort." *Mackinac Island Film Company.* 2005. 21 February 2006.
http://www.mackinacfilms.com/mra.html.

Ignatius, John-Paul Brother.
"Seven Types of Ghosts: A Catholic, Biblical Perspective." *Online Spiritual Warfare Center.* 2001. September 17, 2003.
http://www.oswc.org/FurtherStudy/SevenTypes.asp.

KickingDog.
"Mackinac Island." *Ghostzoo.* October 3, 2003. Feb. 22, 2005.
http://www.ghostzoo.com/forum/partagium/viewthread.php?tid=116&page=1.

Kissick, Brian.
"Ste. Anne's Parish Website." *Ste. Anne's Parish Website.* 20 September 2005. 5 December 2005.
http://www.geocities.com/steanne2000/.

London 24.
"Encounters (Metivier Inn)." *TripAdvisor.* 13 March 2006. 13 March 2006.
http://www.tripadvisor.com/ShowTopic-g42423-i351-k240238-l2423361-Mackinac_Island_Michigan.html#2423361.

Maritime Heritage Program.
"Waugoshance Light." *Maritime Heritage Program.* 19 April 2002. 9 August 2003. http://www.cr.nps.gov/maritime/light.

"Matthew Geary House (Mackinac Island)." *Wikipedia.* June 28, 2006. June 30, 2006. http://en.wikipedia.org/wiki/Matthew _Geary_House.

"Metivier Inn." *Metivier Inn.* 22 February 2006. 22 February 2006. http://www.metivierinn.com/.

msubutterfly55.
"Mackinac Island." *Ghostzoo.* Feb. 22, 2006. http://www.ghostzoo.com/forum/partagium/viewthread.php?tid=116&page=2.

Nirbhao
"some of my favorite Mackinac Island ghost stories." *Livejournal.* October 2, 2005. November 8, 2005.
http://nirbhao.livejournal.com/580298.html.

offcel.
"Mackinac Island." *Ghostzoo.* March 2, 2006. Feb. 22, 2006. http://www.ghostzoo.com/forum/partagium/viewthread.php?tid=116&page=2.

Portella, Javier.
"Moral Re-Armament." *Religiousmovements.* 12 December 2000. 3 March 2004.
http://religiousmovements.lib.virginia.edu/nrms/moralrearm.html.

Roesch, Brian.
"Ghost Ships of The Great Lakes." *Webspawner.* 2 February 2000. 28 August 2003. http://www.webspawner.com/users/ghostshipsofthegreat/.

Roesch, Brian.
"Pine Cottage Investigation." *Webspawner.* 23 March, 2000. 28 18 June,
2003. http://www.webspawner.com/users/pinecottageinvestiga/.

SkiFreak.
"Great Lakes ghost ship stories." *Ghostplace.com.* 24 June 2004. 12
August 2004.
http://www.ghostplace.com/forum/topic.asp?TOPIC_ID=6263.

Scott.
"Dreambook For Mackinac Island." *Dreambook.* August 5, 2002. Sept.
10, 2003. http://books.dreambook.com/mintshady/mac.html.
Jody. "Dreambook For Mackinac Island." *Dreambook.* July 19, 2002.
Sept. 10, 2003. http://books.dreambook.com/mintshady/mac.html.

State of Michigan.
"Labor and Economic Growth". *Michigan.gov.* May 8, 2005.
May 10, 2006.
http://www.dleg.state.mi.us/bcs_corp/image.asp?FILE_TYPE=MAN&FI
LE_NAME=R200506%5C2005166%5C00001646.tif

"Stonecliffe History." *The Inn At Stonecliffe.* April 6, 2004. August 27,
2004. http://www.theinnatstonecliffe.com/history.html.

Southwest Ghost Hunter's Association.
"Ghost Types Defined." *Southwest Ghost Hunter's Association.* April
19, 2006. http://www.sgha.net/ghost_types.html

Taylor, Troy.
"Common Places To Find Ghosts." *American Ghost Society.* 2004. May
6, 2005. http://www.prairieghosts.com/common.html.

Taylor, Troy.
"Interviewing The Witness." *American Ghost Society.* 2004. May 6,
2005. http://www.prairieghosts.com/interview.html.

Taylor, Troy.
"Researching Haunted History." *American Ghost Society.* 2004. May 6, 2005. http://www.prairieghosts.com/hist.html.

Taylor, Troy.
"Small Point Cottage Investigation." *Webspawner.* 2 February 2000. 28 August 2003. http://www.webspawner.com/users/smallpointcottageinv.

The Island House Hotel.
"The Island House Hotel History". *The Island House Hotel.* May 7, 2006. May 7, 2006. http://www.theislandhouse.com/

"The Shadowlands Ghosts And Hauntings." *Shadowlands.* April 1, 2006. April 19, 2006. http://theshadowlands.net/ghost/.
Warren, Joshua P.. *How To Hunt Ghosts : A Practical Guide.* Simon & Schuster. New York. 2003.

thetaxlady.
"Encounters (Metivier Inn)." *TripAdvisor.* 13 March 2006. 13 March 2006.
http://www.tripadvisor.com/ShowTopic-g42423-i351-k240238-l2423361-Mackinac_Island_Michigan.html#2423361.

Thomas.
"Dreambook For Mackinac Island." *Dreambook.* June 6, 2002. Sept. 10, 2003. http://books.dreambook.com/mintshady/mac.html.

Thomas.
"Dreambook For Mackinac Island." *Dreambook.* Nov. 12, 2002. Sept. 10, 2003. http://books.dreambook.com/mintshady/mac.html.
Thomas.
"Dreambook For Mackinac Island." *Dreambook.* 12 September 2002. 12 August 2004. http://books.dreambook.com/mintshady/mac.html.

Welker, Glenn.
"Arch Rock On Mackinac Island." *Indigenous People's Literature.* 9 September 1998. 1 October 2004.
http://www.indians.org/welker/archrock.htm.

Waugoshance Lighthouse Preservation Society.
"Our Lighthouse." *Waugoshance Lighthouse Preservation Society.* 9
August 2003. http://www.waugoshance.org/ourlighthouse.htm.

Other Sources

A Promise For Zoe. (Date & Author Unknown).

Busch, Jane C.
National Historic Landmark Nomination , Mackinac Island [PDF file].
(2000).

Kingma, Lorraine.
Chateau Lorraine: Victorian Bed and Breakfast. [Brochure]. (2003).

Library of Mchigan.
1870 Census. [PDF file].(1870).

Mackinac State Park Commission. (2003). *Fort Mackinac* [Brochure].
Mackinac Island, Mich.

Additional Ordering Information

Thank you for purchasing *Haunts of Mackinac*. For additional copies, please send inquiries to:

E-mail:
　　　　orders@hauntsofmackinac.com

Mailing Address:
　　　　House of Hawthorne Publishing
　　　　P.O. Box 36985
　　　　Grosse Pointe, MI 48236 U.S.A.

The price of each book ordered is
Book Price:　　$14.95 per book
Tax:　　　　　$　.90 per book (Michigan Orders)
Shipping:　　　$ 2.00 per book
　　　　　　　$17.85 total per book ordered

Please make sure to include the following information to speed your order along:
- Your Full Name
- Address
- Telephone Number
- E-mail Address
- The Quantity of Books You Want To Order
- Payment

Thanks Again!

More From Haunts of Mackinac

If you are looking for more information and/or photographs, please visit us on the web at:

www.hauntsofmackinac.com

The website is designed to share Mackinac region ghost stories and photographs. So please feel free to visit and if you share a ghost story, tragic tale, or legend of Mackinac, we may include it in the next edition of *Haunts of Mackinac.*

If you have any questions or comments for the Author please send them to:

E-mail Address: todd@hauntsofmackinac.com

Mailing Address: House of Hawthorne Publishing
Attn: Todd Clements
P.O. Box 36985
Grosse Pointe, MI 48236